Readings from the National Center Test for English

センター英語の長文を読もう

Level 4
(2000-word)

IBC パブリッシング

はじめに

ラダーシリーズは、「はしご（ladder）」を使って一歩一歩上を目指すように、学習者の実力に合わせ、無理なくステップアップできるよう開発された英文リーダーのシリーズです。

リーディング力をつけるためには、繰り返したくさん読むこと、いわゆる「多読」がもっとも効果的な学習法であると言われています。多読では、「1.速く 2.訳さず英語のまま 3.なるべく辞書を使わず」に読むことが大切です。スピードを計るなど、速く読むよう心がけましょう（たとえばTOEIC®テストの音声スピードはおよそ1分間に150語です）。そして1語ずつ訳すのではなく、英語を英語のまま理解するくせをつけるようにします。こうして読み続けるうちに語感がついてきて、だんだんと英語が理解できるようになるのです。まずは、ラダーシリーズの中からあなたのレベルに合った本を選び、少しずつ英文に慣れ親しんでください。たくさんの本を手にとるうちに、英文書がすらすら読めるようになってくるはずです。

《**本シリーズの特徴**》
- 中学校レベルから中級者レベルまで5段階に分かれています。自分に合ったレベルからスタートしてください。
- クラシックから現代文学、ノンフィクション、ビジネスと幅広いジャンルを扱っています。あなたの興味に合わせてタイトルを選べます。
- 巻末のワードリストで、いつでもどこでも単語の意味を確認できます。
- カバーにヘッドホーンマークのついているタイトルは、オーディオ・サポートがあります。ウェブから購入／ダウンロードし、リスニング教材としても併用できます。

《使用語彙について》
レベル1：中学校で学習する単語約1000語
レベル2：レベル1の単語＋使用頻度の高い単語約300語
レベル3：レベル1の単語＋使用頻度の高い単語約600語
レベル4：レベル1の単語＋使用頻度の高い単語約1000語
レベル5：語彙制限なし

CONTENTS

1. Japan Tourist Attractions 2
2. Vinegar—What Exactly Is? 5
3. Rainforest Protection Laws 7
4. Taipei 101 10
5. Soft Drinks 12
6. Dot Game 15
7. Almost an Accident 18
8. Effective Communication with the Elderly 21
9. Fairtrade 24
10. My Role Models 27
11. Picking Up Friends 30
12. Video Games 34
13. Allergy 37
14. Volunteer 40
15. Diet 44

CONTENTS

16. Outdoor Environment 47

17. Holidays of Workers 50

18. Conductors of Heat 54

19. Barbecue 57

20. Internet Search Program 61

21. Eating Habits 64

22. Sign Language 68

23. Animal Tracks 72

24. Friendship—Quality or Quantity? 76

25. Dress Code 80

26. Stereo Set 84

27. International Travel 88

28. TV Station 92

29. The Class e-Times 96

30. Stress 100

31. Preferred Hairstyles	104
32. Ideas about Childhood and Youth	108
33. My Neighbor	113
34. Make a Friend	118
35. Brazilian and Japanese	123
36. Piano	128
37. Monolingual Dictionary	133
38. IT Revolution	139
39. Snowflake	145
40. My Camp Memory	150
41. The Rocks	155
Word List	160

はじめに

　いまの大学受験生はセンター試験で毎年どのような問題を解いているのでしょうか。

　1979年から実施されてきた共通一次試験に変わり、1990年、第1回の大学入試センター試験が始まりました。その内容は、年々変わっています。

　センター試験の長文問題には、大人が読んでもためになったり、興味深く読めるストーリーやエッセイがたくさん出題されています。本書では、2001年〜2010年に実施されたセンター本試験10年分の長文問題を厳選し読みやすい形にして収録しました。

　内容もバラエティーに富んでいます。「日本の観光名所（2010）」「フェアトレード（2009）」「清涼飲料の話（2007）」「アレルギー（2006）」「効果的なダイエット（2005）」といった社会的なエッセイから、「英英辞典（2009）」「スノーフレーク（2007）」「私の隣人（2006）」といったちょっといい話まで、全部で41編を収録しています。

　単語はほとんど現在の高校生が習うものを使っており、語彙レベルは2000語程度となっています。巻末に本文中の全ての単語を収録した辞書形式の単語リストを掲載していますので、わからない単語が出てきた際に参照してください。

———————————————————————————————————— あらすじ

〈あらすじ〉

1. Japan Tourist Attractions 「日本の観光名所」(245語)

　日本で観光名所と言えば、富士山や京都がまず浮かびますが、最近は多様化が進んでいます。最近の調査では温泉や魚市場、アニメキャラなどが観光目的の上位に上げられます。(2010年、第4問A)

2. Vinegar, What Exactly Is? 「酢、その実体とは」(266語)

　世界中で酢は調味料として広くつかわれていますが、酢とは本当のところ一体何なのでしょうか。また料理以外にどのように使われているのでしょうか。(2010年、第3問C)

3. Rainforest Protection Laws 「熱帯雨林保護法」(272語)

　全世界的に熱帯雨林が著しく減少しています。しかし熱帯雨林は人類が生き残っていくために絶対に必要です。ブラジルでは今世紀初頭により強力な熱帯雨林保護法を導入しました。(2009年、第4問)

4. Taipei 101 「台北101」(237語)

　今台北（タイペイ）でもっとも印象的なのは、世界の超高層ビルのひとつである台北101でしょう。内部を地階から順を追って紹介します。(2007年、第3問C)

5. Soft Drinks 「清涼飲料の話」(250語)

　1987年以来、日本で売られる清涼飲料の人気は著しく変化してきました。80年代は炭酸飲料がトップでしたが、現在では緑茶飲料に首位が交代しています。(2007年、第4問A)

6. Dot Game 「ドット・ゲーム」(278語)

　キャロルとトモは、学校の食堂で昼食を終えたあと、次の授業の始まる前に、キャロルが覚えた新しいゲームをすることにしました。(2007年、第5問B)

7. Almost an Accident 「あわや衝突事故」(356語)

　4車線道路の先の交差点で、スポーツカーがトラックを追い抜きながら赤信号で無理な左折をしようとしたその瞬間、交差点右手から突然バ

あらすじ

ンが飛び出してきました。(2010年、第5問)

8. Effective Communication with the Elderly 「高齢者との効果的なコミュニケーション」(375語)

今日の討論は、若い人が高齢者とどのようにコミュニケーションをとるべきかです。パネリストは医師のマクドナルド先生、老人学専門のジョンソン氏とウエスト女史の3名です。(2010年、第3問B)

9. Fairtrade 「フェアトレード」(392語)

イギリスのガースタングという町では「フェアトレード」商品の販売を奨励しています。「フェアトレード」商品は、一般の商品と一体どこが違っているのでしょうか。(2009年、第3問C)

10. My Role Models 「模範にしている人」(352語)

私が模範にする2人を紹介します。2人とも世界に貢献し、世界をよりよい場所にするために自分の能力を使う思いやりのある人たちです。(2008年、第3問C)

11. Picking Up Friends 「友人の出迎え」(328語)

アンナは、迎えにいく予定の2人の友人がほぼ同じ時間に別の場所に着くことになってしまったので、千津子に電話して協力を求めました。(2007年、第5問A)

12. Video Games 「テレビゲーム」(334語)

テレビゲームに魅了される若者が増加しています。テレビゲームが10代の若者に与える影響について、皆さんの意見を伺いたいと思います。(2007年、第3問B)

13. Allergy 「アレルギー」(330語)

近年、アレルギーで苦しむ子供たちが増えています。都会の子どもだけでなく田舎の子供たちにも多く発生しています。清潔過ぎる環境が原因ではないかとも言われています。(2006年、第3問C)

14. Volunteer 「ボランティア」(371語)

日本でも少しずつボランティア活動に対する認識が高まってきましたが、欧米よりもまだかなり低いと言わざるを得ません。国内でも地域差

がかなり見られるようです。(2006年、第4問)

15. Diet 「効果的なダイエット」(307語)

多くの人たちが痩せようとしていますが、カロリーを減らすだけのダイエットはあまり効果がありません。運動や他の身体活動と組み合わせる事で効果的なダイエットができるのです。(2005年、第3問C)

16. Outdoor Environment 「戸外の環境」(303語)

子ネコや子イヌが遊びながら生きる方法を学ぶのと同様に、人間の子どもも遊びを通して生きる方法を学びます。しかし現代の日本には子どもたちが遊べる戸外の環境が少なくなっています。(2004年、第3問C)

17. Holidays of Workers 「労働者の休日」(363語)

日本人は他の先進国と比べてどのくらい熱心に働いているのか、どのくらい休みをとっているのでしょうか。アメリカ、イギリス、フランス、ドイツと比較しました。(2004年、第4問)

18. Conductors of Heat 「熱の伝導」(343語)

冬に毛皮のコートを着る人がいますが、毛皮そのものが暖かいわけではありません。毛皮は暖めてくれるのではなく、保温してくれているのです。(2003年、第3問C)

19. Barbecue 「バーベキュー」(364語)

テリー、パット、アンディの3人がキャンプ地に到着しました。テントの設営場所やどこでバーベキューをやるかを話しています。蚊も出てきました。(2003年、第5問)

20. Internet Search Program 「インターネット・サーチ」(347語)

調べたいことがある時に、インターネット上で検索するのはとても便利です。本棚に百科事典を置く必要もなくなりました。しかし良いことばかりとは言えないようです。(2002年、第3問C)

21. Eating Habits 「食習慣」(358語)

国際カロリー協会の研究者が、世界中の5都市で子供たちが毎日の食事からとるカロリー量の調査を行いました。子供たちのカロリーの取り方は都市によってさまざまでした。(2002年、第4問)

あらすじ

22. Sign Language 「手話」(379語)

英国で勉強している高校生の由美子と友人のポールが駅で会って手話の話になりました。由美子が習った手話は、アメリカ人のポールが知っているものとは違っていました。(2002年、第5問)

23. Animal Tracks 「動物の足跡」(369語)

アンと絵里が森にハイキングに出かけて、いろいろな動物の足跡を見つけます。アンは、それぞれの足跡がどの動物のものかを絵里に教えます。(2001年、第5問)

24. Friendship—Quality or Quantity? 「友情について」(442語)

できるだけ多くの人と友達になるのがよいのか、少なくても仲の良い友達を持つ方がよいのか、友情の質と量について授業で討論しました。(2009年、第3問B)

25. Dress Code 「服装規定について」(444語)

今週のSpeak outコラムでは、私たちの学校における強制的な服装規定の必要性について3人の生徒たちの意見を紹介しています。(2008年、第3問B)

26. Stereo Set 「ステレオセット」(465語)

オーエンは友人たちと買い物に出かけて大きなステレオセットを購入しましたが、すぐに仕事に行かなければなりません。友人たちが彼の車まで持って行くと言ってくれました。(2006年、第5問)

27. International Travel 「国際観光」(430語)

観光産業は国際貿易の重要な一部となっています。中国、ドイツ、日本、メキシコ、スペインの6ヶ国で国際観光の収支について比較してみました。(2005年、第4問)

28. TV Station 「テレビ局」(470語)

小学生たちがテレビ局に見学に訪れました。今スタジオではショー番組の録画を放送しているかたわらで、地元の天気予報の生放送の準備をしています。(2005年、第5問)

29. The Class e-Times 「オンライン学級新聞」(428語)

有希とジェリーは、オンライン学級新聞『The Class e-Times』のためのHPを作っていて、掲載する記事の内容や写真、レイアウトについて話し合いをしています。(2004年、第5問)

30. Stress 「仕事とストレス」(407語)

看護士、航空管制官、プログラマ、中学校教師という4種類の職業で働く人々に対して、ストレスが与える影響と、ストレス解消の方法についてそれぞれリサーチしました。(2003年、第4問)

31. Preferred Hairstyles 「好まれるヘアスタイル」(435語)

年代ごとに流行した5種類の男性ヘアファッションについて、10代後半、30代後半、50代後半の異なる年齢層の人々がどのように考えているかという調査がカナダで行われました。(2001年、第4問)

32. Ideas about Childhood and Youth 「子ども時代と青年期」(656語)

今日では、子ども時代や青年期が人格形成に重要だとされ、大人自身までもが若者の影響を受けています。しかしこのような考え方になったのはわりと最近の事なのです。(2010年、第6問)

33. My Neighbor 「私の隣人」(692語)

奇妙で怖い老人、というのが私の子供時代に隣に住んでいたピールさんの印象でした。ところが大学の食堂で彼を知る人に偶然出会い、ピールさんへの見方が大きく変わります。(2006年、第6問)

34. Make a Friend 「友だちになる」(693語)

水泳の全国大会の選考を控えたバタフライ選手の私の前にアンジェラという強力なライバルが現れます。リレーチームでバタフライの空きは1人分しかありませんでした。(2004年、第6問)

35. Brazilian and Japanese 「ブラジル人と日本人」(665語)

私は7歳のときにブラジルから日本に引っ越して来ました。小学校では、友だちもできて楽しくやってきました。しかし中学に入ったときに問題が起こります。(2003年、第6問)

あらすじ

36. Piano 「ピアノ」(650語)
　私は8歳からピアノを始めました。才能を認められた私はやがてプロのピアニストを目指して音楽学校に入学します。そんな私に初めての演奏会の機会が訪れます。(2002年、第6問)

37. Monolingual Dictionary 「英英辞典」(778語)
　私が大学に入学したとき、翻訳者のおばが辞典をプレゼントしてくれたのですが、それは英語だけで書かれた英英辞典でした。おばはなぜ私にそのような辞典をくれたのでしょうか。(2009年、第6問)

38. IT Revolution 「IT革命」(761語)
　私の姪のアンは、最近就職活動を始めましたが、この数年で人々の仕事の仕方がIT革命により大きく変化したことを彼女は知りました。(2008年、第6問)

39. Snowflake 「スノーフレーク」(760語)
　白髪の老人が、翌日友人とヨーロッパ旅行に出かける予定の孫娘ヴァレリーに、昔、初めておばあさんとバルセルナへ旅行に行ったときの思い出を話します。(2007年、第6問)

40. My Camp Memory 「キャンプの思い出」(726語)
　私が大学生だったころ、夏は中学生のサマーキャンプの手伝いをしていました。その時の思い出の中で特に印象深かったのは、ある少年との出会いでした。(2005年、第6問)

41. The Rocks 「入江の大岩」(738語)
　ジェリーは海岸の入江の岩場に泳いで行くと、そこには何人かの年上の男の子たちがいました。一番大きい子が水中に飛び込むと、その子はいつまでも浮かんできませんでした。(2001年、第6問)

Readings from the National Center Test for English

1. Japan Tourist Attractions

Mt. Fuji and Kyoto have traditionally been popular sightseeing spots for overseas tourists to Japan. However, as the number of incoming tourists increases, their reasons for coming to Japan seem to be diversifying as they develop new interests. A recent survey by the Japan National Tourist Organization (JNTO) lists hot springs, fish markets and *anime* characters among the top ten reasons for visiting Japan, as shown in the graph below.

The top place was taken by Japanese cuisine, mentioned by 71% of the respondents, with traditional architecture and gardens in second and third places. Modern architecture was also mentioned (by 28% of the tourists asked). Hot springs resorts and *ryokan* inns, long enjoyed by

1. Japan Tourist Attractions

Japanese people, have now caught the attention of foreign tourists, too, and both of these are among the five most popular types of attractions. *Sumo* and other traditional sports also feature prominently on the list. Tokyo's Tsukiji fish market has been a draw for visitors to Japan for a number of years, but now it is joined by places like Akihabara, which sell goods related to *anime* characters.

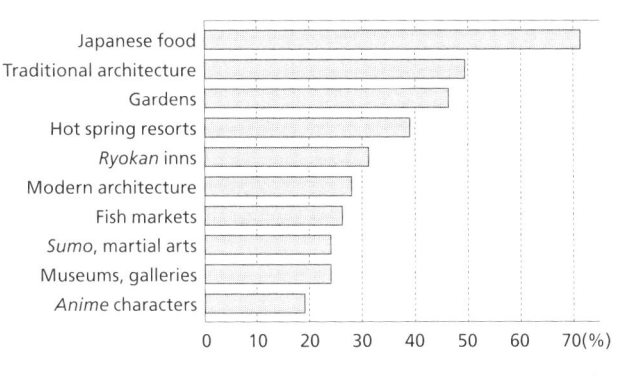

Japan's main attractions for foreign tourists

(Data: Japan National Tourist Organization, 2007)

One reason for the increased variety of tourist hot spots appears to be the greater availability of information, not only in the long-established form of guidebooks but also through websites, especially those catering to specific interests. Tour guides report that many visitors now arrive in Japan with a clear idea of where they want to go and what they want to see.

2. Vinegar—What Exactly Is?

Vinegar is a very familiar household product, which has long played an extremely important part in cooking all over the world. But what exactly is vinegar and what are its uses besides cooking?

People in different places make vinegar out of their local products. In Japan, rice is used to make vinegar, which is a necessary ingredient in making some traditional Japanese dishes. In Korea, they use another native crop, persimmons; in the U.S., apples; and in the Philippines, sugar cane. It is clear that there is a variety of vinegars worldwide.

Regarding the process of making vinegar, it is made by allowing air to react with alcohol of some type. This means that the the process always begins with a raw material, such as grapes, rice, or hops, that has been converted into alcohol. Vinegar can be produced either by a slow or fast process. The former, allowing it to age naturally, can take weeks or months, or even in an extreme case, as long as 100 years, as in expensive Italian balsamic vinegars. The latter process can take as little as 20 hours. This is made possible by adding air and bacteria to the source liquid.

The uses of vinegar are as extensive as its source materials. Before refrigerators became common, vinegar was vitally important in preserving food in the form of pickles. Vinegar has also long been important in cleaning and for medical purposes. It has been commonly used to polish surfaces and reduce the pain of insect bites. Clearly, vinegar was an important discovery for ancient civilizations which remains useful even today.

3. Rainforest Protection Laws

Scientists estimate that eight thousand years ago rainforests covered approximately 60 million square kilometers of the Earth's surface. Due to human destruction only about 35 million square kilometers now remain. Even this relatively small area contains more than half of the world's estimated 10 million species of plants, animals and insects. The diversity is so great that scientists have, until now, succeeded in studying less than one percent of the species living there.

Native people who live in rainforests depend on them for food and shelter. Because trees have been cut down and burned, native people, unable to find enough food, have starved. Additionally, they have been killed or forced out of the rainforests by outsiders who have seized land for profit. The population of native people in the Brazilian rainforest, for example, has decreased over the past 500 years from approximately 6 million to 200,000.

Rainforests are destroyed to make money from selling not only trees but also cattle and crops that are raised on the cleared land. However, experts say that rainforests will have more economic value if we leave them as they are and harvest their medicinal plants, oil-producing plants and

Annual Loss of the Brazilian Rainforest
1989–2006

3. Rainforest Protection Laws

fruits. This knowledge, plus the fact that native life is becoming extinct, led Brazil to introduce stronger rainforest protection laws at the beginning of this century. These laws aim to protect native tribes, prevent illegal cutting of trees and expand the protected rainforest area. All countries that are contributing to the destruction of rainforests should begin their own efforts to protect them. Rainforests are essential to human survival. Therefore, we are all responsible for protecting this biological treasure.

4. Taipei 101

Taipei has many things to be proud of, but perhaps the most impressive is the L-shaped Taipei 101 Mall. At 508 meters, it is one of the world's tallest buildings. Taipei may not be widely known for its modern architecture, but it does have this towering building. The building has become a symbol of Taipei's progress, identity and vision.

Let's start in the basement and work our way up. There we can see the Grand Market, Asia's largest food court. We then move up to the first floor where a busy shopping mall begins. On the second and third floors we find a variety of designer shops, while the fourth floor, called City Square, offers coffee shops with tables in a central plaza. On the fifth floor, we can buy tickets for

4. Taipei 101

the elevators to the observation deck. They are the world's fastest, and in no time at all we are at the top of the building. Half a kilometer below, the scene glows orange-pink with city lights. Even after the sun sets, we can still make out the outline of Taipei's surrounding mountains, blacker than the evening sky.

Taipei 101 represents the progress of Taipei and its identity. By visiting this building, one can sense the attractiveness of this modern city. Of course, many other aspects of Taipei's culture are appealing, too. However, the citizens of this city can be proud to have this impressive building.

5. Soft Drinks

What do you like to drink when you get thirsty? Since 1987, the popularity of different types of packaged soft drinks in Japan has changed considerably. During the late 80s, carbonated drinks of all sorts (such as sodas and colas) were the leaders in popularity, with fruit juices a close second and coffee-based drinks a bit further back in the competition. By 2004, however, those drinks had lost their lead to the newest entry into this market: tea-based drinks of all types. Tea drinks, which include green teas, took the lead over both carbonated drinks and coffee-based drinks. The total production of tea-based drinks was nearly double that of the nearest competitors: carbonated drinks and coffee drinks. Fruit juices had fallen to fourth in

5. Soft Drinks

popularity with a drop in production of nearly one fourth since their highest levels in the late 80s. Fifth place was held by sports drinks, which in 1987 were in fourth place ahead of tea drinks.

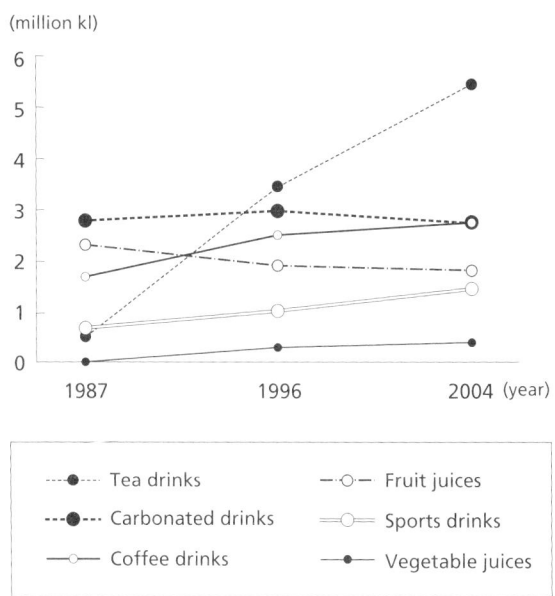

Production of Packaged Soft Drinks

(データ：全国清涼飲料工業会、『清涼飲料関係統計資料』 2005)

At about the same time that green tea became a packaged product, vegetable juices also began to appear on the market. They have had a very small but relatively consistent place in the market since then.

One of the reasons for the popularity of tea-based drinks might be that many people like to have a non-sweetened green tea drink with the rice balls that they buy at convenience stores. Many other types of packaged soft drinks contain some amount of sugar which doesn't really fit people's taste when eating rice.

6. Dot Game

Carol and Tomo are in the school cafeteria. They've just finished lunch and have a little time before their next class begins.

CAROL: I've just learned a new game. Would you like to try it?

TOMO: Sure.

CAROL: I have a clean sheet of paper, so all you need is a pencil.

She marks three dots on the paper with her pencil.

CAROL: The game begins with these dots. Actually, you can start with any number of dots. But, at first, it's best to start with three or four.

She adds another dot on the paper.

Tomo: Where on the paper do we mark the dots?

Carol: You can place them anywhere you like. Now, join any two dots with a line. Players take turns drawing a line.

She joins two dots that are next to each other with a curved line.

Tomo: Don't you have to draw a straight line?

Carol: No. Any kind of line will do. In fact, you can even make a loop starting and ending at the same dot. But you can't draw a line that crosses itself, or any other line.

Tomo: O.K. And?

Carol: When you've drawn a line, put a new dot somewhere on it. Each dot may have only three lines connected to it. So, since a new dot placed on a line already has two lines connected to it, it can only have one more.

6. Dot Game

Tomo: I see. Are there any other rules?

Carol: No. That's it. You continue playing until you can't draw another line.

Tomo: And the player who draws the last line is the winner?

Carol: Exactly. Now that you understand the rules, let's play!

7. Almost an Accident

Witness A: I was standing at the bus stop opposite the gas station on Route 300, a four-lane road. That had always been a dangerous area, but it's safer now because they recently put in traffic signals. There were two vehicles on the road approaching the signal. One was a small farm truck and the other a brand-new sports car. It was getting dark but the heavy rain had just stopped and there were no other cars around. Anyway, the truck and the sports car were driving side by side when the car started to swerve from side to side. I think the truck may have moved slightly to stay away from the car, but I'm not sure—I couldn't take my eyes off the car. The signal was red, but instead of slowing down, the car sped ahead rapidly. The driver was going to

7. Almost an Accident

go through the intersection when the light was red! And that's when a van suddenly came into the intersection from the side. It looked like they were going to hit, but they both turned away from each other at the last second and avoided a crash. But then the back doors of the van opened up and hundreds of soccer balls spilled out.

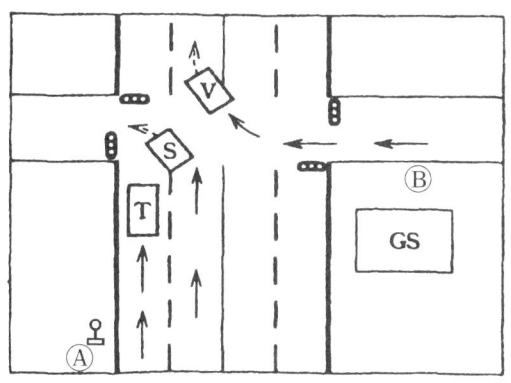

Ⓐ = witness A   Ⓑ = witness B   GS = gas station
T = small farm truck   S = sports car   V = van   ⚑ = bus stop

WITNESS B: I was walking on the side road toward Route 300—coming to the intersection. I noticed that they had put up signals near the service station. This should help make the intersection safer. Suddenly, a van came up from behind me. It was strange—I could see inside the van and it was full of soccer balls! I had never seen anything like that before. Anyway, as the van was approaching the signal, the light turned from green to yellow. But the driver went faster when he should have slowed down—he drove into the intersection where he almost hit a sports car. It was so lucky—the man was able to turn to the right and miss the car. I think the sports car turned too. Fortunately, there was no accident, but there were soccer balls all over the place.

8. Effective Communication with the Elderly

CHAIR: Today's discussion is about how younger people should communicate with the elderly. We invited three panelists: Dr. McDonald, a medical doctor, and Mr. Johnson and Ms. West, who are researchers specializing in gerontology, or the study of the elderly. Mr. Johnson, can you start our discussion?

MR. JOHNSON: Certainly. I often notice people communicate in a particular way with the elderly. People exaggerate their ways of speaking, for instance, by using a loud voice. Sometimes people speak as if they were talking to a child, but I wonder if older people really like this. In my observations at senior centers, even doctors and nurses employ this particular way of speaking. However, I wonder if this is a good way to communicate with them.

CHAIR: That's an interesting observation. You're saying that medical professionals also speak differently to the elderly. What do you think, Dr. McDonald?

DR. McDONALD: Well, as doctors, we have to be considerate when we talk to patients. We should adjust how we communicate with older people to make sure they understand what we say. Often, they can't hear well, so it's important to speak to them slowly and clearly. They need to understand us, so they can respond to questions we may have. I'm sure they're grateful when they're addressed in this manner. I feel that when you meet a person who appears to be old, you should always show consideration by speaking in such a manner.

CHAIR: OK. Dr. McDonald, with his professional

experience, thinks that special attention should be paid to the elderly. What are your thoughts on this point, Ms. West?

Ms. West: I'm an older person myself, but I'm afraid I have to disagree with Dr. McDonald. He said he could tell who needs to be spoken to clearly and slowly from their appearance. I guess you base your judgment of older people on their slow movements, gray hair, and wrinkles. But that's a stereotype of the elderly. Some older people may not need any special adjustments during conversation. Rather, such adjustments may insult them. I don't want to be addressed like that, or stereotyped in that way.

Chair: Thank you. Ms. West's comments emphasize that our judgments of the elderly shouldn't be made without careful consideration.

9. Fairtrade

It has been said that nine out of ten people like chocolate and the tenth one is lying, but did you ever think about who gets the money you pay for your favorite chocolate? In fact, the farmer who grows the cocoa beans and the farmer whose cows give the milk get very little of the money you pay. Most of it goes to the companies which transport the raw materials, turn them into chocolate, then package, advertise and distribute it to stores. As a result, the cocoa and milk producers often live in very poor conditions. One small town in England is trying to change this situation.

Garstang, near Lancaster in England, is a town which encourages stores to sell "Fairtrade" goods; in fact, it calls itself "The World's First Fairtrade Town." If you buy goods with the

9. Fairtrade

"Fairtrade" label, you can be sure that a reasonable part of the money you pay will go to the farmer who grows the raw materials from which your goods are made. For example, money paid for "Fairtrade" chocolate goes to cocoa farmers in Africa. People in Garstang became interested in "Fairtrade" when they began to look for a way to help these farmers. The farmers complained that big chocolate companies were interested only in buying cocoa beans inexpensively, and not in whether the farmers had enough money to live. One group in Garstang decided to buy cocoa directly from the farmers and make it into chocolate, making sure the farmers could keep as much of the profit as possible.

The chocolate sold in stores in Garstang with a special "Fairtrade" logo on it was more expensive than ordinary chocolate, but 82% of local people said they were willing to pay extra if they knew the money was being used to help people in a poor country. Gradually, other goods came to be traded in this way.

The next thing that happened was that local dairy farmers demonstrated in the center of Garstang. They wanted to become involved in the "Fairtrade" movement. They pointed out that, like the cocoa farmers in Africa, they also felt disadvantaged by an unfair trading system. They wanted more money for the milk their cows produced. As a result, Garstang has become a center not only for fair trade with poorer countries, but also for promoting locally produced goods.

10. My Role Models

A role model is an ideal person whom we admire. Role models may have various backgrounds and ways of looking at things. However, they all inspire others through their actions. I would like to introduce two people I admire.

Mr. Chico Mendes is one of my role models. He was born in the Amazon region in 1944 to a poor Brazilian family that had farmed rubber from rubber trees for many generations. They loved the rainforest and used its resources in a way that did not destroy it. However, mining companies and cattle ranchers started destroying the Amazon rainforest which is more than 180 million years old. They burned and cut down hundreds of thousands of trees, endangering the living environment of the people there. Chico began a movement that organized ordinary workers to oppose those harmful practices. The movement eventually spread to other parts of the world, as Chico's efforts led people in other countries to protect the earth's forests and the forests' native inhabitants. Mr. Chico Mendes is a role model for me because of his courage, dedication and self-sacrificing work to protect not only the Amazon rainforest, but the natural environment of the entire planet.

Dr. Mae Jemison, the first Afro-American female astronaut to travel into space, is my other role model. Mae was born into a middle-class American family. She entered university at the age of 16, and went on to receive degrees in Chemical Engineering, African-American Studies and Medicine. She became a fluent speaker of Japanese, Russian and Swahili. In 1992, she was the science mission specialist on the space shuttle Endeavour, on a cooperative

10. My Role Models

mission between the U.S. and Japan. A compassionate person, Dr. Jemison has used her education to improve the lives of others by providing primary medical care to poor people. She has helped countless people through various educational and medical projects.

The main characteristics of my two role models are that they sympathize with other people's distress and are committed to improving the world by helping others. They are caring people who use their potential to benefit the world, making it a better place.

11. Picking Up Friends

Anna telephones her friend, Chizuko, to ask her for help.

Anna: Hi, Chizuko. This is Anna.

Chizuko: Hi. Tomorrow is the day you and your friends are coming to Hakata, right?

Anna: Yes, but I have a little problem.

Chizuko: What's wrong?

Anna: Well, Moon Suk is coming as planned. But Jin Ah waited until the last minute to buy her ticket. So, when she tried to get a ticket to Shimonoseki, the ship was fully booked.

Chizuko: Oh, no . . .

Anna: Luckily, she was able to get a ticket to Hakata. The problem is, they'll arrive at

11. Picking Up Friends

about the same time.

Chizuko: So, you want me to pick up Jin Ah?

Anna: Can you do that?

Chizuko: Sure, I'll be happy to meet her.

Anna: Great! Then, I'll meet Moon Suk in Shimonoseki and we'll drive to Hakata to join you.

Chizuko: What time will Jin Ah arrive?

Anna: At 8 a.m. on the Cosmos Line ferry.

Chizuko: At 8 a.m. No problem. How will we recognize each other?

Anna: Jin Ah will call me from Pusan this evening, so at that time I can let her know that you'll be meeting her and I'll tell her what you look like. What do you plan to wear tomorrow?

Chizuko: Hmmm . . . you know my flowered pants?

Anna: The ones with roses?

Chizuko: No, the ones with sunflowers.

Anna: They're really loose, right?

Chizuko: No. Tight.

Anna: Oh, yeah. You wore them last month when we went shopping in Tenjin.

Chizuko: Right. I'll wear those. I'll also have on a straw hat with a wide brim.

11. Picking Up Friends

Anna: Does it have any decoration on it?

Chizuko: Yes. It has a plain ribbon tied around it. Also, I'll be carrying a magazine.

Anna: Great! She can't miss you. Thanks a million. Shall we all meet at the Sakura Hotel tomorrow around 11 a.m.? The four of us can have lunch together.

Chizuko: Sounds good. Drive safely.

Anna: I will. See you soon!

12. Video Games

Moderator: More and more young people are fascinated by video games. These games influence teenagers both positively and negatively. Today, I would like to invite your opinions on this topic.

Brian: Thank you. I'd like to express my views on video games. Sometimes, teenagers who enjoy playing video games seem likely to attempt the tricks that they see. This could lead to serious injuries. On the other hand, playing certain video games allows people to gain skill in using their eyes and hands at the same time. Having such skills can help young people increase their enjoyment of sports activities.

Moderator: So, Brian, you are saying that video games are helpful in improving physical

12. Video Games

responses.

Madoka: It is true that some video games have cool characters who perform neat tricks, and kids try to imitate them. But I think video games could also influence teenagers in a positive way. I've read some studies which say that playing video games encourages you to try harder and achieve more. For example, when you're playing a game and you lose, you might keep on trying to master it until you succeed.

Moderator: You and Brian have offered different opinions. Okay, Madoka, your view is that video games help you learn to never give up.

Moderator: Are there any other views which we should consider?

Joe: Video games definitely influence some teenagers in bad ways. There was an incident in which two teenagers were found with a rifle in their home. They had used it to shoot at trucks passing by, and had killed a man. It seems that they were influenced by a video game. Parents should check the content of video games before buying them for their children. They need to take an active role in determining what their children are allowed to play.

MODERATOR: Thank you, Joe. You have mentioned one negative aspect of video games. What you said is that video games may make children imitate improper behavior, so parents should choose games carefully.

13. Allergy

The past thirty to forty years have seen a huge increase in the number of children who suffer from allergies, and scientists are still looking for the explanation. Some have blamed increased air pollution, but it has also been found that allergies are common not only among children in the city but also among children in the countryside, where pollution is typically much lower.

A currently popular explanation for the rise in allergies is the so-called "hygiene hypothesis." The basic idea is that young children brought up in an environment which is too clean are more at risk of developing allergies. Nowadays, people bathe and wash their clothes more frequently than in the past, and thanks to vacuum cleaners homes are less dusty, too. One result of all these changes is that in their early lives children are exposed to fewer allergens—substances that can cause allergies—and this means that their bodies cannot build up natural immunity to them. Simply put, exposure to allergy-causing substances is necessary for natural protection against them to develop.

The trend towards smaller families also means that young children encounter fewer allergens in the home. In fact, it is known that children who have older brothers and sisters are more resistant to allergies. The same is true of children who share their home with a pet. Such children are much less likely to develop the very common allergy to cat or dog hair, for example.

Scientists agree that being exposed to a wider range of allergens early in life helps children to develop greater immunity. There is, however, also some data suggesting that genetics, family income, and even the parents' level of education may play a part in how likely a child is to suffer from allergies. Thus, although the hygiene hypothesis is an important area for research, we cannot yet be sure that too much attention to cleanliness is the only explanation for the enormous rise in the number of allergy victims.

14. Volunteer

"Heaven helps those who help themselves," said Benjamin Franklin. Although we are familiar with the message contained in this old saying, the fact remains that we have to help each other. And that is what hundreds of millions of people are doing—working as volunteers. In 2001, 28.9 percent of Japanese citizens volunteered their services. This number suggests that the idea of volunteering is becoming more attractive, because in 1983 a similar survey on that topic found that only 20 percent had some experience with volunteering. Even so, that percentage was lower than for the United States and the United Kingdom, where more than 50 percent of citizens had some experience of volunteering.

Differences can be found within a country as

14. VOLUNTEER

well. The graph below shows regional variations with respect to volunteer activities among four prefectures in Japan in 2001. As mentioned above, the overall rate of participation of Japanese in community service was 28.9 percent. In that year Hyogo appeared to be typical of the nation in regard to that rate. The leading prefecture was Kagoshima, where more than 40 percent of the people had some volunteer experience. Yamanashi's rate was similar to that of Kagoshima, but preferences differed when it came to types of volunteer work: A little over 10 percent of the volunteer work focused on community safety, compared with 7.4 percent in Kagoshima.

Those living in Tokyo seemed to be less involved in volunteer work than the nation as a whole. In fact, the overall percentage was the second lowest of all the prefectures in Japan. Furthermore, the nation's capital had the lowest

Participation Rates: Regional Comparison of Volunteer Activities

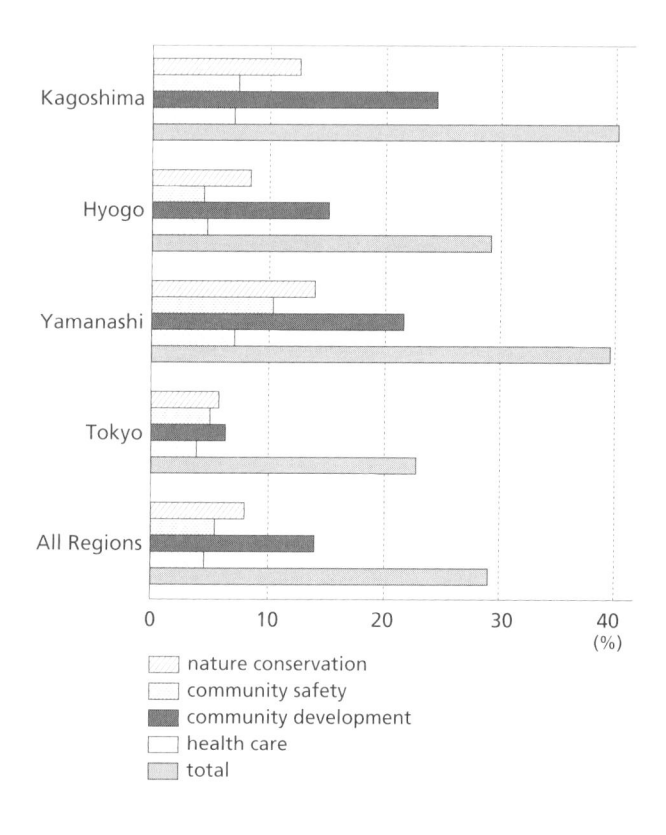

- nature conservation
- community safety
- community development
- health care
- total

(Data：総務省, *Survey on Time Use and Leisure Activities*, 2001)

percentage in community development. It might be that people living in big cities see themselves as individuals and not as members of a community. Or, perhaps they simply do not have time to think of their neighbors.

The Japanese government has been making efforts to establish a system to promote volunteer activities. Indeed, Japan was the driving force behind the United Nations making 2001 the "International Year of the Volunteer." Although variations among and within countries will likely continue for quite some time, it is hoped that government support for this important activity will encourage more people to help their neighbors and their communities.

15. Diet

These days many people are trying to lose weight. Dieting will help, but there is some evidence that cutting calories alone is not the best way to become, and stay, slimmer.

Studies show that a weight-loss program that relies only on dieting is less effective than a plan that includes physical exercise. One expert claims that people who cut 250 calories through dieting can double that number by combining it with exercise and other physical activities. However, forget the common belief that you have to suffer in order to make progress. Exercise need not be uncomfortable. For people who favor an aerobic program, cycling and swimming are good activities. Dancing can also slim you down.

Some researchers have suggested that part

15. Diet

of the added physical activity should be in the form of weight training. Their study involved two groups of women. Both were dieting, but one group also lifted weights while the other did not. The women in both groups lost 13 pounds on average, but the weight-training women lost *only* fat. The women who did not lift weights lost not only fat but also muscle. Yet another study, however, found that overweight people on low-fat diets who increased or changed their regular daily activities—by choosing the stairs over the elevator, for example—were better able to maintain weight loss than those in a tough physical program. This is perhaps because lifestyle changes are easier to stick with than exercise programs for which you must set aside time.

How can you put these findings to use right now? There are a lot of ways to do so. Stand up, walk, stretch . . . . These are just a few of the things you can do immediately, anywhere, and without any equipment. So go for a walk during your coffee break! You'll feel better and be healthier as a result.

16. Outdoor Environment

When we watch kittens and puppies playing, we realize that through play they are learning how to live. They learn various physical skills, such as how to jump over barriers without getting hurt. They also learn social interaction. For example, if a kitten bites his sister too hard, she will get angry and bite him back. These physical and social skills form part of the training that young animals need in order to grow up.

Just as kittens and puppies learn about how to live through play, so do children. But in present-day Japan, especially in cities, there is not much space for children to play in. Children need to release their energy for their mental and physical health. They need space, especially outdoors, so that they can run, jump, and yell.

Another point to consider is how much time children have to play. Some people say that four to five hours a day of playing outdoors with others is necessary, even for twelve-year-olds. It is very doubtful, however, whether any Japanese children get that much free time. Concerned about their future in an increasingly competitive society, parents generally tell their children to study more; very few would tell them to go out and play.

What do these children do at home when they are not studying? They tend to spend time by themselves. They play video games or watch TV, for instance. These activities do not teach them how to get along with others. This can only be learned through playing with other children. They need to play without being told what to do by adults in order to learn about leadership and group harmony on their own. Outdoor space is particularly suitable for this purpose. Children need a proper outdoor environment where they can freely spend their time playing with friends.

17. Holidays of Workers

How hard do Japanese people work? Do they have enough free time to enjoy family life, travel, or hobbies? We have compared the working hours and holidays of workers in the manufacturing industry of five nations for the year 1995.

There are national holidays in each of the five countries, and people often enjoy three-day weekends. Japan leads this group in terms of the number of national holidays per year, with 15 days on its calendar such as Children's Day and Culture Day.

What if we look at the total number of holidays per year? This would include not only national holidays but also weekends and paid vacation. Germany led the five nations in the total number of annual holidays with 157 days. France came in second with 154 days. The United Kingdom (UK) was third, followed by the United States of America (USA). Japan came in last with the smallest number of holidays.

Some people say that the Japanese are taking more time off than they used to, and that the number of Japanese vacationing overseas is high. This may be true, but statistics show that, in 1995 at least, Western Europeans and Americans took more holidays than the Japanese did.

Most Western Europeans take about four weeks of paid vacation a year, while the Japanese and Americans usually take much less than that. A problem that seems to be unique to the Japanese is that only a small percentage of the paid vacation offered is actually taken. There are a lot of Japanese who do not feel comfortable about taking time off while their fellow workers have to continue working. Some Japanese business leaders, however, have encouraged workers to take more paid vacations in an effort to reduce international criticism that the Japanese work too hard.

Annual Working Hours and Holidays (1995)

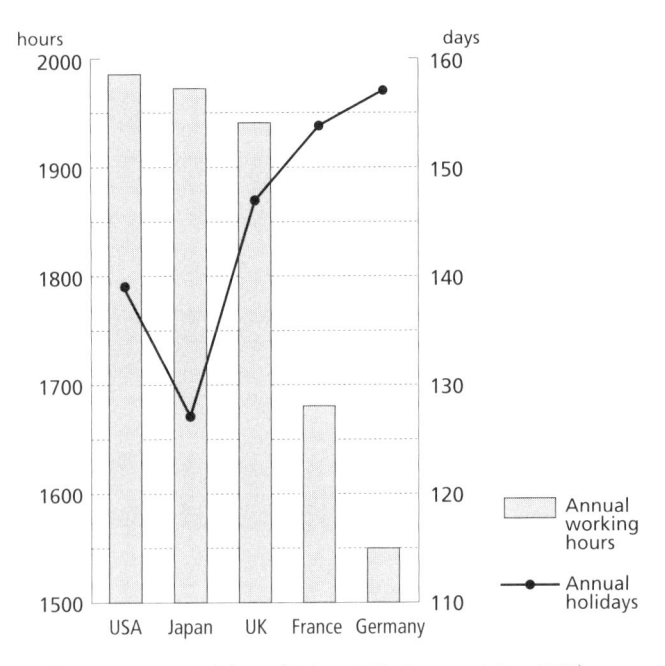

(Data: Japanese Ministry of Labor, *White Paper on Labor*, 1997)

17. Holidays of Workers

Surprisingly, Japan came in second to the USA in terms of the average number of annual working hours at 1,975 hours in 1995. The United Kingdom came in third at 1,943 hours, followed by France at 1,680 hours. Germans worked the fewest hours that year. It is interesting that research such as this shows that facts do not always match the impression most people have.

18. Conductors of Heat

Some people wear a fur coat for warmth in winter, but few realize that the fur in itself is not really warm at all. In fact, it has the same temperature as its environment. It does not warm us but keeps us warm. The source of heat is our body, not the fur. Fur is specially suited to preserving body heat by preventing it from flowing off into the cold surroundings. In other words, fur does not let heat pass through it easily: it is a poor conductor of heat.

Different materials conduct heat differently. A frying pan with an iron handle soon gets too hot to be touched. This is because iron allows heat to pass through it very quickly. We prefer our frying pans to have wooden handles since wood is a poor heat conductor. Similarly, air does not

18. Conductors of Heat

conduct heat as well as water. We would find a room of 22°C quite comfortable even if we wore just a swimsuit, while bath water of the same temperature is unpleasantly cool. The water takes heat from our warm body much more quickly than the air does.

Different parts of our body conduct heat differently. This can be easily proved. An object that is too hot to be touched for more than a second with our hands or lips can be in contact with a fingernail for some time. That is because a fingernail is a poor conductor of heat and the heat only reaches the sensitive layer under the nail gradually.

Hair and feathers consist of materials similar to nails. They, too, are poor conductors of heat and so a very good protection against cold. In addition to this feature, they keep a layer of air underneath. So geese, hares, and even bears in Siberia do not need special winter coats. They have been given warm coats by Nature. Humans, having only a very small amount of natural hair, have hunted birds and animals for their feathers and fur since ancient times, and we still use feather bedcovers and wool blankets.

19. Barbecue

Terry, Pat, and Andy have arrived at a campground.

TERRY: Let's set up the tent before we get the barbecue going.

ANDY: Yeah, we'd better do that. Why don't we put it close to the lake near the camping sign? We'll have to have the entrance facing away from the lake, though, to keep the wind out.

TERRY: I don't think we need to. It's not so windy. If we set it up facing the lake, we'll get a nice view.

ANDY: OK, let's do that.

Later, after setting up the tent . . .

ANDY: Now, where should we put the barbecue?

TERRY: How about behind the tent?

PAT: All right. If we put it near the water tap, it'll be easy to wash the vegetables.

ANDY: That's not a good idea. It's kind of muddy over there.

TERRY: Yeah, you're right. How about in front of the tent?

PAT: But that would block the entrance. I know, why don't we put it at the side? That way it's still not too far from the water tap.

ANDY: If you say so. You're the boss, Pat. Terry, can you get the barbecue ready while I go and get the things from the car? I'll be back in a few minutes.

TERRY: OK . . . . Ouch! I'm getting bitten. There seem to be lots of mosquitos down here

19. Barbecue

by the lake. Have you seen the insect spray anywhere, Pat?

PAT: I think Andy had it. I remember he said something earlier about getting bitten.

TERRY: Did you see where he put it?

PAT: Maybe by the camping sign?

TERRY: I don't see it there. He must have put it away somewhere.

PAT: Oh, now I remember. He put it in one of the backpacks.

TERRY: Which one?

PAT: The big one.

Terry: Where in the backpack?

Pat: In the side pocket.

Terry: The side pocket? Which one, top or bottom?

Pat: The bottom one.

Terry: Let's see . . . . No, I can't find it. Are you sure it was this backpack?

Pat: Oh, sorry, it must have been the other one.

Terry: The other one? Ah, yes, here it is, but it's in the top pocket. You'd better put some on, too, and then we can start getting the vegetables ready.

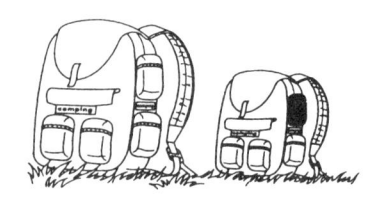

20. Internet Search Program

What would you do if you wanted to learn about something? A traditional way is to go to your bookshelf, pick up a dictionary or encyclopedia, and start turning pages. Now, however, you can turn on your computer, connect it to the Internet and start its search program. You just type in the keyword(s), click "search", and soon you will have what you are looking for.

It seems as if anything you want to know can be found on the Internet. The range of information you can find on the Net varies from gossip, to news, to the most advanced technological findings. Furthermore, the information is always fresh. New information is constantly added, past files are re-written, and news reports are broadcast as they come in. It seems we do not need to "know" or "remember" anything except how to get information from the Net. Or at least, there is no longer any need for the shelf space to hold those volumes of encyclopedias.

What is being lost, though, is the joy of discovery. In many ways an Internet search is like a package tour, on which you generally know where you are going and see only what the tour organizer has selected. Similarly, what you find in the Internet search is controlled by the site's owner or is the result of a computer program. On the other hand, turning the pages of an encyclopedia, as you look up an entry, is more like wandering through a forest. You may accidentally find something interesting in the entry just next to the one you have been looking for. This may stir up a new interest, which will eventually lead you into a totally different topic.

The word "encyclopedia" originally meant "general or well-rounded education". With a

20. Internet Search Program

traditional encyclopedia, this well-roundedness may be achieved by the discoveries readers make by turning the pages. In comparison, heading straight to the target word through a series of clicks on a computer is rather linear. This suggests that technological changes in the methods of getting information may limit the opportunities for learning.

21. Eating Habits

Researchers at the International Calorie Association (ICA) have claimed that it is important to develop well-balanced eating habits. Ideally, calories should be taken in equally from three meals: breakfast, lunch, and dinner. They also point out that the recommended daily number of calories for children is from 1,900 to 2,100 kcal.

The researchers carried out a survey intended to measure the number of calories children get from regular meals each day. They chose several primary schools in five cities around the world: Guana, Jamas, Lomita, Norstar, and Portville. Every day for seven days, five hundred primary school children aged 7 to 10 in each of the five cities reported what they ate. Then the ICA

21. Eating Habits

calculated the average number of calories in each meal and in snacks. The results are shown as percentages of the total daily calories in the pie charts below.

The way young children get calories from meals each day varies from city to city. For

Total Calories per Day

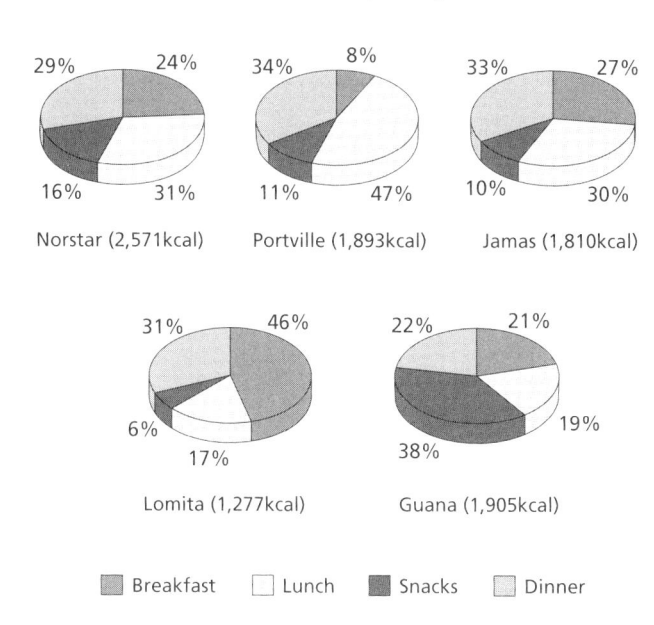

Norstar (2,571kcal): 29%, 24%, 31%, 16%

Portville (1,893kcal): 34%, 8%, 47%, 11%

Jamas (1,810kcal): 33%, 27%, 30%, 10%

Lomita (1,277kcal): 31%, 46%, 17%, 6%

Guana (1,905kcal): 22%, 21%, 19%, 38%

Breakfast   Lunch   Snacks   Dinner

children in Guana, snacks provide the most calories. This may be because they consider snacks as equivalent to a major meal. On the other hand, snacks don't have much importance for children in Lomita. They get most of their daily energy from breakfast. The total amount of energy they get each day is quite small. The eating habits of children in Portville are unique. Many children tend to skip breakfast and have a rather big lunch. In contrast, the diet of children in Jamas is well-balanced. A similar pattern is shown for the children in Norstar. The total number of calories is, however, much greater than the ICA's recommendation. The children's parents will be advised to keep better control over their children's diet even though there is a good balance of calories between the three meals.

The ICA concluded that there are important differences in the ways children around the world get calories, and that they have to take these

21. Eating Habits

differences into account when they give dietary advice to people. The researchers also feel that more surveys are required, so as to discover what kind of diet is needed, since this survey focused only on the number of calories.

22. Sign Language

Yumiko, a high school student studying in Britain, meets her friend, Paul, at the station.

Yumiko: Hi, Paul.

Paul: Hi, Yumiko. What are you doing these days?

Yumiko: I'm learning sign language.

Paul: Sign language? Why are you doing that?

Yumiko: We have a new student in our class who is deaf, and I thought it might be useful. I'm starting a short training course on Monday, so I've learned the sign alphabet to prepare for it. Of course, there's much more to sign language than that, though.

22. Sign Language

PAUL: You know, I learned some alphabet signs when I was in America. My friend showed me a few. His brother is partially deaf. For 'A', you just make a fist like this, don't you?

YUMIKO: Actually, British signs are a bit different.

PAUL: Are they? I didn't know that.

YUMIKO: Yes. In fact there are quite a lot of sign languages. The British and American ones are just two of them.

PAUL: So, what's the difference?

YUMIKO: In British sign language, each vowel—A, E, I, O, U—is made by pointing with the index finger of one hand to one finger of the other hand in turn. So 'A' is the thumb, 'E' is the index finger . . . .

PAUL: I get it. So 'I' is the middle finger, and so on.

YUMIKO: You see, it's easy, isn't it? Some other letters are easy too. For the letter 'X' you just cross both index fingers, and for 'C' you make a half-circle shape with your thumb and index finger. Then 'D' is the same as 'C', except that you close the half-circle with the index finger of your other hand, like a capital 'D'.

PAUL: Really? In the American sign alphabet the letter 'D' is made with one hand, and looks like a small 'd'. What about if I just make a circle with my thumb and index finger? In America, that's 'O', but . . . .

YUMIKO: Yes, remember 'O' is made by pointing to the ring finger in British sign language. There

22. Sign Language

are signs that use a circle, though. For example, for 'P' you make a circle and touch it with the index finger of the other hand in a straight line. Do you see?

Paul: Hmm, I wonder why they're different.

23. Animal Tracks

Ann has invited Eri, a new exchange student, to go hiking in the woods with her.

Ann: Eri, look at these!

Eri: Wow, what are they?

Ann: They're animal tracks.

Eri: Year, I can see that, but what kind of animal?

Ann: A wolf, probably.

Eri: How do you know?

Ann: Well, look at the top half. Can you see the four claws? Also, the main part of the foot makes a triangle-shape. This is typical of wolves.

Eri: Amazing! Wait, Ann, look at these! What

23. Animal Tracks

are they?

ANN: Hmm... I think they're from a type of rabbit.

ERI: Really? They look like a duck's footprints to me.

ANN: Yeah, they do. But ducks' feet don't have rounded toes. They're webbed.

ERI: Webbed?

ANN: Oh, that means the toes are connected by skin—like a frog, for example.

ERI: I see... but the entire shape is like a duck's print.

ANN: Actually, it's shaped like a snowshoe. These prints are from a snowshoe hare.

ERI: Why is it called that? Is it a "hairy" animal?

ANN: No, not that kind of hair! A hare looks like a rabbit. And a snowshoe is a large, flat thing we wear for walking on snow. This type of hare's foot has the same shape, so it's called a snowshoe hare.

ERI: I see.

ANN: Now look at these over here. Can you see any different between these and the first ones we saw?

ERI: Umm. . . they look like a wolf's, but they have five claws, not four.

ANN: Right! These belong to a wolverine, a different animal. The other difference between the footprints is the shape of the main part.

ERI: I see, instead of one big triangle-shape, this one has two separate shapes.

ANN: Also, it's much more rounded at the top, just under the claws. The other ones were more pointed.

23. Animal Tracks

Eri: Gosh, you know so much about this stuff.

Ann: I just picked it up from my uncle. He likes to look for mushrooms in the woods and needs to know what animals are around—just to be on the safe side.

Eri: Wow, I'd like to meet him one day.

24. Friendship—Quality or Quantity?

Teacher: Today, we're going to talk about the issue of friendship. Let me ask a question: Is it better to make friends with many people, or to have just a few good friends? In other words, which is more important, the quantity of our friendships or the quality of our friendships? Does anyone have any comments? Yes, Jordan.

Jordan: I think it's important to have a friend you can count on when you're in trouble. We all have some tough times, and we need someone to talk to at such times. No matter how many friends you have, your problems can't be solved unless you have someone you can trust. Having many friends doesn't always mean that their advice will help you solve your

24. Friendship—Quality or Quantity?

problems. Here at school, I have just two good friends, but I know I can rely on them for anything I need. They both help me a lot in my daily life. I think this is far better than having lots of friends. Also, you can't maintain long-term relationships with many people. The fewer friends you have, the more time you can spend with each of them. Just saying "Hi" to everybody doesn't give you a better quality of life.

TEACHER: OK. Thanks a lot. Jordan says quality is more important than quantity in friendships.

TEACHER: Any other ideas? Amy?

AMY: I think people should have a lot of friends throughout their lives. I mean, you should get on well with as many people as possible because having a lot of friends will widen and deepen your understanding of life in various ways. You'll learn and experience different ways of thinking by knowing them. I like having many friends because each friend brings me new possibilities. Also, I disagree with Jordan. When you're in trouble, fewer friends will give you fewer chances to solve the problem. When I have a problem, I like to ask as many friends as possible for their advice.

Teacher: All right. Amy thinks that the more friends you have, the more chances you'll have to solve problems.

Teacher: Any other comments on this question? Maria?

Maria: Unlike Jordan and Amy, I don't think we have to choose between having "many" friends and having "good" friends. I'm one of Amy's many friends, but that doesn't necessarily mean the quality of

24. Friendship—Quality or Quantity?

our relationship is bad. In fact, she's always good to me, listens to my problems and offers advice, even though, as she says, she has many friends. I believe people can have both.

Teacher: Well, I think that's an excellent way to conclude, Maria. We can have both quantity and quality in our friendships.

25. Dress Code

The topic for this week's "Speak Out" column is whether there should be a mandatory dress code in our school. The first opinion selected was sent in by Monica Molina, a tenth grader. She writes:

There needs to be some limitation to what students can wear to school. Without a dress code students could wear clothing that is offensive, inappropriate, distracting, or threatening. Clothing with offensive slogans and pictures that promote drugs, alcohol and smoking should not be allowed. Pictures and slogans which are offensive to race and gender should not be allowed, either. Clothing with distracting pictures or writing could take students' attention away

25. Dress Code

from studying, which is why students are here. Clothing with messages, writing or pictures that are threatening to students or teachers shouldn't be worn. Being in a school with no dress code would be very bad. A dress code should be made, taking into consideration everyone who studies and works in the school.

Our next opinion was submitted by Kishan Santha, an eleventh grader, who says:

Students should be free to choose what they want to wear to school. Granted, there are some shirts that have offensive writing on them but the majority of messages are not offensive. Most messages do not negatively affect our learning and attention in class. If we have a dress code at all, it should state that students cannot wear clothes with insulting words on them. But, that is it. I'm sure that whether there is a dress code or not, my friends will wear what they know is fine and appropriate in school. Teachers should trust us to be able to determine whether or not the clothes we decide to wear are appropriate.

The third opinion selected was written by Kim Higgins, a twelfth grader. She says:

I believe that students can express themselves with their clothing. However, there should be some kind of dress code at school. It should not be a strict code, but a realistic one that everyone can follow. A rule that I find reasonable is that a shirt or blouse should not be so short that part of the person's body can be seen. It particularly bothers some people when they can see someone else's bare stomach. Also, we should not have to see other people's underwear. This offends some people and can be considered insulting. If we don't have school dress rules, with today's fashion, things could get out of control.

We would like to thank Monica, Kishan and Kim for submitting their opinions to "Speak Out." They have given us a number of important points that we must consider seriously before everyone votes on this policy.

26. Stereo Set

Four university friends are finishing their lunch after shopping in the morning.

Owen: That was an amazing sandwich.

Jay: Well, you ate it so fast I'm surprised you could taste it.

Yuki: He's right. Did you even chew?

Owen: Oh, give me a break. I was hungry. And I have to go to work in a few minutes, so I had to hurry.

Yuki: Yeah, that's right. You have to work. Are you going to take all those boxes and shopping bags with you? That stereo set, for one, is really big.

Owen: But it was so cheap, and it's totally cool. I'm really glad I found it. Don't you think

26. Stereo Set

it's great?

YUKI: Yeah, I do. But you don't have much room in your shop. Is there a place where you can keep it all while you work?

OWEN: Hmm, I don't think so. I wish I'd thought about this earlier because I could have taken all this stuff to my car, but now I don't have time.

JAY: We can take it for you. I know what your car looks like.

OWEN: Thanks. That'd really help me out. But actually, I didn't drive my own car today. Something's wrong with the engine, so my sister lent me hers.

YUKI: What kind of car does she have?

OWEN: It's, it's uh . . .

JAY: Don't you remember?

OWEN: Well, it's white. Oh, and it has four wheels!

JAY: Stop joking. You just described most of the cars in an average parking lot. You'll have to give us more information than that, or we can't help you.

OWEN: Right. Well, it has some bad scratches on the left side, on the driver's side. It's parked in the north lot on the green level, just above the red level. Believe it or not, it's not locked. And my niece's teddy bear is in the front passenger seat.

Their friend Ella returns from the restroom.

OWEN: Hey, Ella. You know my sister's car, don't you?

ELLA: Yeah. Did she ever get the scratches fixed?

OWEN: No, not yet. So let me explain where it's parked. When you get off the escalator into the parking lot, turn right.

26. Stereo Set

Jay: Wait, is that toward the exit?

Owen: Uh, you'll be facing the exit. At the exit, turn left. Then go down to the last row and turn left again. Her car is on the right toward the end of that row. There are some handicapped parking spots opposite it near the elevator.

Yuki: That sounds easy enough.

Jay: OK, you'd better get to work. Give us your stuff.

Owen: Thanks a lot. Oh, please lock the car before you leave it. I don't want to give anyone a chance to steal my new stereo!

Ella: No problem. See you later.

27. International Travel

Tourism is an important part of international trade today, and business activities connected with transportation, hotels, services, and entertainment for tourists are essential sources of income for many countries. The figure below shows the amounts of money earned from and spent on international travel in 2000 by six countries: China, Germany, Japan, Mexico, Spain, and the United States of America (USA).

While the figure shows that the USA led other countries in both earning and spending, we can also see that nations receiving large sums of money from tourism do not always spend equally great amounts overseas. For example, the amount of money spent by Spanish travelers abroad was less than 20 percent of that earned from

27. INTERNATIONAL TRAVEL

foreign travelers to Spain. China also earned more from international tourism than it spent. The opposite pattern was shown by Germany and Japan, where the amounts spent abroad by their citizens, 47,785 million dollars and 31,886 million dollars, respectively, were far greater than the amounts earned, 18,483 million dollars and 3,373 million dollars.

International Tourism: Amounts Earned and Spent (2000)

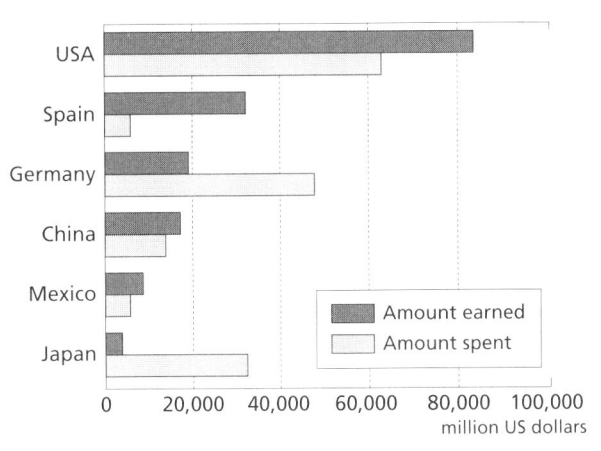

(Data: Ministry of Land, Infrastructure and Transport, *White Paper on Tourism*, 2003)

According to the World Tourism Organization, there is a growing tendency for tourists to seek out places where they have never been. Europe, which received almost 60 percent of all international tourists in 2000, is expected to see its share fall to 46 percent by 2020. On the other hand, by that time the East Asia and Pacific region will have replaced North and South America as the second most popular tourist destination. Of course, tourists choose a destination not only on the basis of how fresh it is or whether an international event such as the Olympics is being held there, but also by the level of safety and the ease of getting around.

Many foreigners have the idea that Japan is too far away and too expensive, and its language and culture too hard to understand. However, distance and language alone cannot explain Japan's lack of appeal to tourists from North America and Europe: in 2000, China received

27. International Travel

more visitors from these areas than Japan did. Despite its negative image among some tourists, many who do make the trip to Japan are pleasantly surprised by the friendliness of its people and the efficiency of its public transportation. Moreover, not every foreign visitor finds Japan so expensive these days. With its safe society and excellent travel facilities—not to mention its history, culture, and natural beauty—there is no reason why Japan should not become one of Asia's major tourist destinations. The amount spent by foreigners in Japan may one day be more than that spent by Japanese overseas.

28. TV Station

Elementary school students are taking a Saturday morning tour of a TV station.

Mr. Wright: Welcome, boys and girls, to WXRP Channel 19. I'm Dan Wright. Today you'll tour the station to find out how we broadcast the programs you watch on TV.

Bobby: Mr. Wright, it's ten o'clock, and I'm usually watching the *Mailman Jack Show* right now. Is Mailman Jack here? Can we see him?

Mr. Wright: Actually, Bobby, our studio is too small for us to do the show here. Instead, Mailman Jack makes a videotape of the show at a bigger studio in Peyton City and sends it to us. We're playing the tape right now, and that's how people can

28. TV Station

> watch it at home. But while that tape is playing, we're getting ready for a live local weather report. Let's go into the studio to watch how we do it.

The students go into the studio and see a woman in front of a blue screen.

Mr. Wright: In 30 minutes, Ms. Cole here will be pointing to different parts of the blue screen behind her and talking about the weather. All you see now is that empty blue screen, but if you look at the TV screen over here, you see something else. Take a look.

Carla: Wow, it's a weather map, and Ms. Cole's standing in front of it!

Ms. Cole: That's right, Carla. This is what people actually see on their TV at home. The map you see now is of our part of the state at eight this morning. Here we are in Jonestown. Here's Lake Axelrod south of us and the Blue Hills to the northwest. Peyton City is northeast.

Carla: What is that letter in the circle next to Peyton City, and that line with black triangles between Jonestown and Peyton City?

Ms. Cole: The line is called a "cold front," and the "R" in the circle stands for rain. It was raining in Peyton City this morning.

Carla: I see. Then a "C" in the circle would mean cloudy, right?

Ms. Cole: That's a good guess, Carla, but no. I'll get to that later.

Bobby: Is it going to rain here?

Ms. Cole: Maybe, because the wind is from the northeast, and it's likely that the cold front will move past Lake Axelrod by this evening. Even if it doesn't rain, it's going to get cooler in Jonestown.

28. TV Station

BOBBY: What about that circle above Jonestown?

MS. COLE: That's a symbol for a sunny sky. When you came in this morning, the sky was clear, right? If it had been cloudy, Carla, the symbol would have been filled in and look like a big black ball. Now, that cold front is still moving toward us, and we can expect a cloudy sky—maybe even rain—in a few hours.

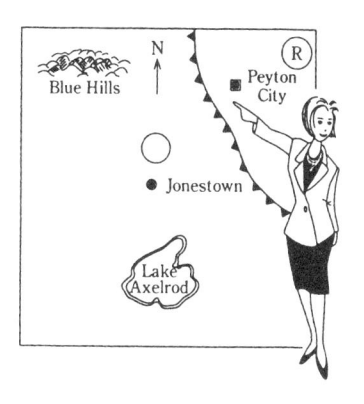

29. The Class e-Times

Yuki and Gerry are making a homepage for their class on-line newspaper, "The Class e-Times."

Yuki: OK, let's check what we've got so far. We've decided to have one main story and one short story, right?

Gerry: Right. And what about pictures? Should we have one for each story?

Yuki: I'm not so sure about that. Maybe it would be too much. How about just for the main story?

Gerry: That sounds good. Now, what will our stories be? We could do one about the students who visited from Korea. Maybe we can use one of the photos they sent us.

Yuki: Mmm, we could do that for the short

29. The Class e-Times

story. I think I'd rather have the bus tour we took to Kyoto as the main story, though. It was a lot of fun, and I'm sure people still remember the trip very clearly.

GERRY: That's a good idea. What about that great story you wrote about the trip for the homework assignment? We can use that as it is, if you could type it into the computer. I can't write about it myself because I missed it.

YUKI: Oh, I remember. You were sick, weren't you?

GERRY: That's right. I wish I could have gone there.

YUKI: It was great. Kinkakuji was beautiful.

GERRY: You must have seen a lot of women in kimono.

YUKI: Not really. And even when we went to Gion later, we only saw a couple of them.

GERRY: Oh, really? Have we got photos of them to go with the story?

YUKI: Yes, I've got a few here on my desk, but we decided we'd have just one picture. Do you think it should go with the story about the Korean students or this one?

GERRY: I think it would be better to use one of your Kyoto photographs. Those pictures came out clearer.

YUKI: You're right. Look, I have this beautiful one of a woman in kimono, and these, here, of Kinkakuji.

GERRY: I like the first one. Can we use that?

YUKI: OK. The only thing now is to decide where to put each story.

GERRY: I've got an idea. We could have the main story in the left column, with the picture next to it at the top, and the Korea story

29. The Class e-Times

under the picture.

Yuki: I like that. It's got good balance. So, it looks like we're almost there. I'm beginning to see the light at the end of the tunnel.

Gerry: Yes. We're getting a pretty dear picture of what the homepage will look like, aren't we?

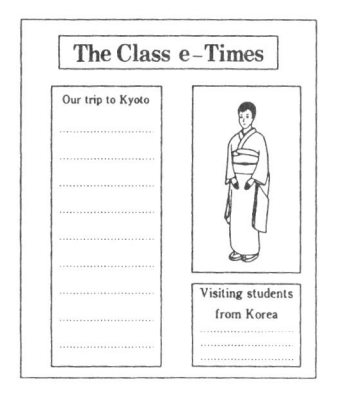

30. Stress

It is well known that stress affects workers' health. When workers are not well, they tend to miss many days of work every year. The organizations they work for are, in turn, not as productive as they should be. However, levels of stress in different occupations, and the ways that workers relieve such stress, have not been studied in depth. The Occupational Psychology Association (OPA), therefore, conducted a survey on the effects of stress on workers in four different occupations and on the methods they use to relieve workplace stress.

The OPA researchers interviewed 100 workers in each of four occupations: nurses, air traffic controllers (ATCs), computer programmers, and junior high school teachers. The workers were asked about the kinds of stress symptoms they had and how they dealt with stressful situations.

The four types of stress symptoms mentioned most often were high blood pressure, overeating, depression, and sleeplessness. The OPA researchers found that workers in the different occupations reported different frequencies of these stress symptoms.

The nurses reported that they ate more when they felt stressed. The ATCs were more affected by high blood pressure than other disorders. Many of the computer programmers tended to feel nervous and anxious. The teachers reported that they could not sleep well.

The researchers found that workers used five main methods to fight stress both at work and at home. They were interested in how these ways of fighting stress differed in the four occupations. The figure below shows how people in the four occupations relieved stress.

The nurses interviewed claimed that talking to others and shopping were the usual ways to relieve stress. They also said that they liked listening to music from time to time. The ATCs claimed that the responsibility for hundreds of lives on the job put a lot of pressure on them. They relieved this stress by shopping or sleeping, and when possible by playing sports. The computer programmers,

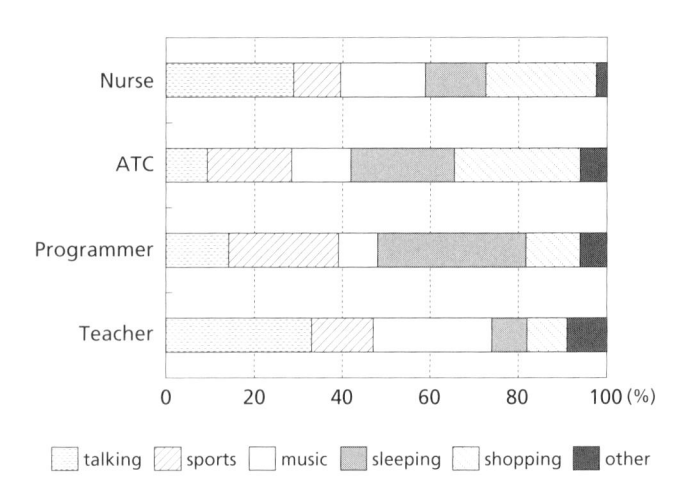

Stress Relief Methods

talking / sports / music / sleeping / shopping / other

on the other hand, preferred sleeping and playing sports as the best ways to escape the effects of any stress. They said that shopping, talking to others, and listening to music were less frequently used methods of stress relief for them. The teachers preferred talking with other teachers as well as listening to music, particularly classical music, as the best ways to relieve stress.

The OPA researchers concluded that workers in different jobs have different types of stress symptoms and employ different ways of relieving stress.

31. Preferred Hairstyles

How do people's preferences for styles change across different generations? In order to investigate how different age groups view hair fashion, a survey was conducted in Canada. The research data were gathered in the following way: People across the country were randomly selected with the use of telephone books. They were called and invited to join the study if they were in their (1) late teens, (2) late thirties, or (3) late fifties. After 600 people agreed to participate, the researchers interviewed them at home, while showing them a series of photographs of male faces, each of which featured a different hairstyle. The researchers were interested in examining how much the three generations favor the following five hairstyles.

31. Preferred Hairstyles

| Crew cut | Rock and roll | Long hair | Bushy | Disco |

Among the five hairstyles was one commonly found in the 1950s. It was called the "crew cut", which was closely clipped hair with a flat top. The style selected to represent the early 1960s was common among rock and roll groups. It featured hair cut evenly across the forehead with just enough to cover half of each ear. Hair that was not cut at all was fashionable in the late 1960s. In this period, hair down to the shoulders was not uncommon. The early 1970s were represented by curled hair which was brushed up into a high, soft and woolly bush. The hairstyle associated with the late 1970s was shorter than that in the early 1970s. The hair was brushed down to cover the ears and the sides of the face. This was the "disco" style.

The charts below indicate the percentages of each hairstyle chosen by people in the three age groups.

Two major findings came out of the survey. The first one was that particular hairstyles were preferred to varying degrees. The crew cut was popular in all three groups. The least favored hairstyle, in contrast, was the "bushy" style. The disco style was chosen as the second most favored

Preferred Hairstyles

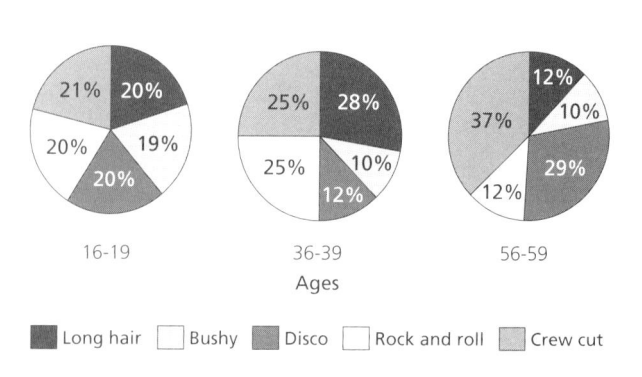

Ages 16-19	Ages 36-39	Ages 56-59
21%, 20%, 19%, 20%, 20%	25%, 28%, 10%, 12%, 25%	12%, 10%, 29%, 12%, 37%

■ Long hair ☐ Bushy ■ Disco ☐ Rock and roll ■ Crew cut

31. Preferred Hairstyles

hairstyle by the oldest group, although this style was not so popular among people in their late thirties. Long hair turned out to be unpopular among people in their late fifties.

The second finding of the survey was that older people preferred a more limited range of styles. Each of the five hairstyles was selected by more or less equal percentages of those in their late teens, probably reflecting the varied lifestyles of young people. In the case of people in their late thirties, however, there was a strong preference for three styles. This tendency to favor fewer styles is more clearly seen in the oldest group, who for the most part preferred two hairstyles.

32. Ideas about Childhood and Youth

Today, we believe that essential aspects of character are formed in childhood and adolescence. We understand the young have different needs and experience the world differently from adults. We can even see that adults themselves have been influenced by a modern emphasis on youth. However, historically this wasn't always so. The development of modern industrial societies has brought about a fundamental change in ideas about childhood and youth.

As the historian Philippe Ariès has pointed out, modern attitudes towards childhood and youth stand in contrast to views of the young in earlier periods. Ariès has noted that many Europeans in the Middle Ages did not know

32. Ideas about Childhood and Youth

when they were born or how old they actually were. The idea that one becomes an "adult" when one turns a certain age (for example, on one's twentieth birthday) did not exit. Thus, the difference between childhood and adulthood was not clear, and children were often treated in the same way as adults. In medieval France, few children went to school and six-year-olds worked in the fields alongside their elders. Ariès even suggests that the concept of childhood itself did not exit in the Middle Ages.

How did modern perceptions of childhood and youth develop? One important factor was the growth of trade and the rise of merchant cities, as happened in Renaissance Italy. The importance of providing the young with the skills necessary for trade was recognized by cities like Venice and Florence, which set up schools to teach reading, writing, and mathematics. As European nation-states emerged in the seventeenth century, the need for government officials—tax collectors, record keepers, and administrators—expanded. In France under Louis XIV, for example, increasing numbers of young people studied in the many academies created to meet this demand. The trend towards more education continued into the eighteenth century. By the late eighteenth century most children were going to school and spending more time apart from adults.

The increasing numbers of students receiving education brought about another important change of attitude. Eighteenth-century thinkers like Jean-Jacques Rousseau believed children should be allowed to develop according to their individual abilities and not be overly disciplined. Followers of Rousseau, like Johann Heinrich Pestalozzi, stressed the need for play if children were to grow into healthy adults. This emphasis on the needs of children led in turn to further changes. By the middle of the nineteenth century, industrial societies began passing laws to end child labor.

A final factor has been the rise of "youth culture." The development of new technologies in the twentieth century meant a need for greater skills and rapid growth of secondary and higher education. By 1930, a majority of teenagers in America were enrolled in high school; by 1960, more than forty percent of American high school graduates were going on to university. As the time between childhood and adulthood became longer, psychologists emphasized the importance of "adolescence," a period when individuals are most open to the world and make crucial decisions about their futures. But as the young spent more time with their peers, youth developed a culture—music, fashion, even language—independent of adult society.

Present-day ideas about childhood and youth have undoubtedly had an effect on adults.

Movies, television, and music are increasingly aimed at the young and have influenced society as a whole. Many adults imitate the young. They wear clothing—jeans and T-shirts—associated with youth, and try to keep their youthful looks.

Adults have become like adolescents in another way. While technological change creates new products and jobs, this process also means that skills which adults have learned may become out of date. Adults can find themselves in the same position as adolescents: they must be ready to make decisions about their futures, learn new skills or start new jobs. Attitudes associated with adolescence, such as a willingness to explore new options, are increasingly common among adults.

33. My Neighbor

While I was growing up in our small town, Rosemont, I always thought of my neighbor, Mr. Peal, as a strange and somewhat frightening old man. He was always yelling at me and my playmates to stay away from his yard and his old truck. My parents never said much about Mr. Peal and only told me to leave him alone, so I never had any reason to believe he was anything more than an unpleasant old man.

But sometimes, at times and places we least expect, we learn something new about people that changes how we look at them. Such a thing happened to me last year at my university, a hundred miles from home.

One day I was in the cafeteria talking with a classmate about my hometown. Suddenly a student who was sitting next to us interrupted and said, "Did you say you come from Rosemont? Do you know an old man named Peal there? He drove an old blue truck."

"Why, yes," I answered. "He's my neighbor. Do you know him?"

"I do! What a coincidence!" said the student and he began to tell me a story. He told me that he lived in Sunnydale, where the university is, and that one day seven years ago he, his mother, and his little sister decided to spend a day in the mountains near my hometown. "We had to take a train to Rosemont early in the morning, and then a bus from there into the mountains," he said.

He said that he and his sister began using rocks to make a small pool in a mountain stream. "We wanted to catch baby fish and collect them in the pool so that the three of us could watch them swim around for a while before we let them

33. My Neighbor

escape back into the river."

He was arranging one of the rocks in the wall when suddenly his sister accidentally dropped a large rock right on top of his left hand. It cut his fingers to the bone and made a terrible wound. "It hurt so much, and it looked awful," he said. "Mom wrapped my hand in a towel and told us we had to find a doctor."

But the bus back into town was not due for another four hours. The three decided they would have to walk down the road back to town. However, that too, would take more than an hour. "My mother kept telling me to be brave, but I could tell that she was really worried. We were all scared."

Just then, a small blue truck came up the road in front of them.

"Mom started waving and yelling, and the truck stopped. She explained what had happened and asked the driver, an old man, if he would take us into town to see a doctor."

But the man told her that the doctor was out of town and that the only other doctor in the area was another thirty miles away on the other side of Rosemont. "He told us to hop in and that there was some ice for my hand in a bucket in the truck."

The student continued his story, telling me that he could not remember much about the trip to the doctor. However, when he finally walked out of the doctor's room with his fingers bandaged, Mr. Peal was sitting in the waiting room with his mother and sister.

"He said he would drive us back to Rosemont so we could catch the last train home. On the way back he told us that he had no grandchildren, but that his next-door neighbors had a daughter named Sarah around my age, so he knew how Mom must have felt. You must be Sarah, I guess. When you see Mr. Peal again, tell him that I'm

33. My Neighbor

majoring in music—guitar! My hand is perfectly fine."

"I'll do that," I answered.

Our university is large, and I never again met the student who had told me this story. But I did see Mr. Peal again. I see him with new eyes now, and I am glad I have a neighbor like him.

34. Make a Friend

My confidence as a swimmer started to disappear the day Angela moved to our small town. At the time, some members of the town's swimming club, myself included, were preparing for the National Championships, which were just six months away. I had always been the best, and everyone thought that I would be chosen for the relay race. But now I had competition. There was only one place for the butterfly on the relay team, and we both wanted it.

For two weeks it was awful. Angela was always the star. She was faster than I, and her form was better, too. I was jealous and scared. My chances of being selected were disappearing fast. My fear caused me to be unfriendly to Angela. I refused to speak to her and never said anything good

34. Make a Friend

about her.

One day, however, our coach called me over and said, "Kate, I've got something to say to you. Your attitude is hurting your performance. I know you can change that. I'd like you to think about it."

When I arrived at the pool the next morning, I thought about what he had said as I was going through my warm-up. Angela and I were going to compete that morning, and only eight girls would enter the finals.

My thoughts were interrupted when a voice said, "Nervous?" It was Angela. "I don't like to talk before a race," I replied coldly.

"I get nervous, too," she said. Her voice didn't have the anger of mine, which surprised me quite a bit.

Angela and I competed in our separate trial races. I jumped into the pool and swam like a flying fish. My mind was clear, and I could think about only one thing: swimming well.

When the races were over, the judges announced that both of us were among the lucky eight who would be competing in the finals. Despite this good news, I noticed that Angela was sitting sadly alone. This puzzled me, but I thought that I knew how she felt and tried to be friendly to her.

"I don't talk before races, but I do talk *after* them. Sometimes it helps," I said.

Angela was silent for a while, but then she said, "I'm great in practices, but in competitions I just can't do well. It's like this all the time. I'm so worried about the finals."

Now I felt really bad. I realized how horrible I had been to Angela. I wanted to help her. I wanted to show her that I was sorry for my behavior of the past two weeks.

"Listen, I have an idea," I said. "Why don't we help each other prepare for the final race? We

34. Make a Friend

have two weeks to work on things."

"Good idea," said Angela.

For the next two weeks Angela and I worked together. I taught her how to deal with stress and how to train her muscles. She helped me with my form, and at the end of those two weeks we were the best of friends and respected each other as swimmers.

The day of the final race came and when the starter pistol was fired, I swam off like a dolphin. I thought about nothing but winning, but just before I reached the finish line, I thought of Angela and looked over into her lane.

As I was climbing out of the pool, I said to myself, "Oh no, what have I done?" I thought that I had dropped behind Angela and lost the race when I looked in her direction.

While we were waiting for the official announcement, the coach came running over to us. "Congratulations, girls! It was close, but Angela has won, and so have *you*, Kate!"

"What do you mean?" I asked.

"Well, Angela will be in the relay, but you swam so fast, Kate, that you, too, have won."

"Really?" I screamed. "I don't understand."

"I'll explain. The 21st Century Swimsuit Company is giving both of you their Future Swimmers Scholarship this year."

"Wow, I suppose that I'm a double winner: I got a scholarship and made a friend, too."

"You're not the only one," Angela remarked.

35. Brazilian and Japanese

"When are you going back to Brazil?"

I looked down at the ground, trying to stop the tears. I didn't want to cry in front of those two girls. Why did they have to say things like that?

"If only I could go back to Brazil," I thought. Memories of my early years filled my head. Playing, swimming, dancing, music, laughter. . . . When my parents decided to move to Japan, though, I had to leave all that behind. I was only seven years old at the time, but I still remember that day.

"Elena, we're going to Japan."

"For a holiday?" I knew I had some distant relatives in Japan, although I'd never met them.

It would be fun to fly in an airplane and visit them.

"No, to live. We're going to work there, and you'll be able to go to a new school and learn Japanese. Then you'll be able to go to a university there, and if you can speak two languages fluently when you grow up, you'll be able to get a good job in the future."

"I don't want to go to a new school. I like my school here. And what about my friends?"

"Don't worry, Elena. You'll make new friends."

I didn't want new friends. I wanted my old friends, my grandparents, my aunts and uncles, and cousins in Brazil. But there was no arguing; it was decided and that was that. Two months later, we arrived in Japan. The first few months were hard because I didn't speak Japanese. However, my teachers and classmates were kind. I soon picked up the language and made friends

35. Brazilian and Japanese

and spent five happy years at elementary school.

The problems began when I moved to junior high school. My junior high school accepts students from three different elementary schools, and I found myself in a class with many people I had never met before. Although I spoke Japanese fluently and my behavior was in no way different from anyone else's, two of my new classmates started to tease me after they heard me speaking Portuguese with my parents at the entrance ceremony. What hurt me most deeply was the question of when I was going back to Brazil. If I went back to school in Brazil, it would be so difficult to catch up with my former classmates there. Besides, all my friends were in Japan now. I'd spent half my life in Japan, and Japan was my home.

The two girls started again, "When are you going back to Brazil?"

I wished they would stop. Then suddenly, I heard a voice behind me, "Elena, what's the matter?" Natsumi, Maiko, and Kaori were walking over to me. They had been my friends since my arrival in Japan. At first, we taught each other words in Japanese and Portuguese. After that, we always encouraged and helped each other.

"Oh, nothing. I'm just being asked again when I'm going back to Brazil."

Natsumi turned angrily toward the two girls who were teasing me. "Don't you understand? You have only one culture, but Elena has two. OK, that makes her different, but aren't we all different?"

Maiko joined in, saying to the two girls, "You're both different from me, but that's not a bad thing. I'm certainly not nasty to you because of it."

The two girls looked ashamed. After a few moments of tense silence, they walked off toward

35. Brazilian and Japanese

the classroom. As I saw them walking away, the anger inside me overflowed, "I hate it! I hate it!"

Natsumi put her hand on my shoulder, as if to calm me.

"Elena, they just don't understand yet. They'll realize eventually."

"Natsumi's right," added Kaori. "I know that sometimes being Brazilian *and* Japanese makes things difficult for you, but it also makes you special."

"Yes, that's something to be proud of," said Maiko.

My friends were right. Deep inside, I knew that they were right. I looked at them with gratitude and finally let the tears fall.

36. Piano

When I was an eight-year-old girl, I was taken for my first music lesson. Ms. Grodzinska, the teacher, was a plain, elderly woman and her apartment was thick with dust. But in the corner stood a magnificent grand piano, and when Ms. Grodzinska sat down to play a simple melody for me, I was amazed to hear such beauty come from under her fingers. As she played, she altered from a plain woman to someone whose movements were as harmonious as the sounds she was creating. I knew at once that I wanted to be able to bring forth sounds like that.

Piano lessons were part of my parents' ambition for me to have the better things in life. Musicians in Poland have sacred status, and having musical talent is an avenue of success open

36. Piano

to all. As a first step toward fame, I was taken for a musical hearing test, and felt the shame of failing most of it. Later, though, one of my music teachers told me about the importance of "inner ear"—the ability to hear feelingly. In this, I turned out to be better.

Of course, like many children, I hated practicing. It was extremely dull to go through the finger exercises endlessly, but as soon as I was given parts of real pieces I learned them with enthusiasm. I didn't wonder about what they should sound like—I seemed to know. Music seemed to me as clear as words. At the end of twelve months of lessons, Ms. Grodzinska said to me, "Eva, you have talent."

It was decided at once that I should train as a professional pianist, and I immediately entered Cracow Music School. It was an old school that combined a basic curriculum with a full musical education. Inside, the atmosphere was warm with the sounds of violins, red-faced kids running around the narrow hallways, and the heat of competition. We wore a uniform, which hid social inequalities, but the degree of everyone's talent was judged constantly.

A performance, of course, was the peak toward which all the students worked. At the end of my first year at music school, I gave my first public performance and I approached it with all the calmness of inexperience. When it was time to play, I felt such joy that I knew nothing could go wrong. I seemed not to be playing but listening to the music as it poured out of my fingers. It was a happy moment.

But it was also the last time that I enjoyed such an innocent calm. From then on performing became more self-conscious, and more difficult. My childish fearlessness had gone and I had to work harder to get the necessary combination of will and relaxation.

36. Piano

The time I worked hardest was shortly before my family moved to Canada, when I was seventeen. Usually, the school resisted making stars of us, but they decided to make an exception to their policy and allowed me to give a whole concert by myself. This was a frightening idea—to get through so many pieces without losing my nerve and concentration—and in preparation I started practicing like mad. I practiced until my fingers hurt. I practiced to make absolutely sure that I wouldn't shame myself. I practiced until my teacher told me to slow down.

I was more terrified than I had ever been as I sat backstage waiting to go on, and I got through the program not in that simple joy of my first performance, but through powerful focusing of mind and will. Afterward, though, I had my full reward. My friends were particularly generous with praise, and, most exciting of all, my classmate's elder pianist-brother came to tell me how well I'd done and kissed me in an unmistakably adult way. For one glorious moment, music, admiration, and romance all came together, just like they're supposed to.

37. Monolingual Dictionary

When I first entered university, my aunt, who is a professional translator, gave me a new English dictionary. I was puzzled to see that it was a monolingual dictionary, which meant that everything was in English. Although it was a dictionary intended for learners, none of my classmates had one and, to be honest, I found it extremely difficult to use at first. I would look up words in the dictionary and still not fully understand the meanings. I was used to the familiar bilingual dictionaries, in which the entries are in English and their equivalents are given in Japanese. I really wondered why my aunt decided to make things so difficult for me. Now, after studying English at university for three years, I understand that monolingual dictionaries play a crucial role in learning a foreign language.

When I started to learn English at the age of ten, I wanted to pick up as much basic vocabulary as possible and created what might be called a simple bilingual "dictionary" for myself. This consisted of English words and their equivalents in Japanese written on cards. I would put the English word on one side of a card and the Japanese equivalent on the other. I found this to be a convenient tool for memorizing basic everyday words.

In high school I was assigned longer texts which had a larger vocabulary, so I started to use a standard English-Japanese bilingual dictionary. Such dictionaries contain a large number of commonly used English words. Each item comes with a pronunciation guide, its equivalents in Japanese, a note on its grammatical functions, and examples of how it is used.

For those working as professional translators

37. Monolingual Dictionary

and interpreters, there are more specialized bilingual dictionaries. My aunt often translates articles submitted to international medical journals, so she uses a bilingual dictionary devoted to medicine. Such dictionaries, available in various fields, tend to omit words like "come" or "go" used in an everyday sense; on the other hand, they contain highly specialized terms not found in standard bilingual dictionaries. For example, in a bilingual medical dictionary, one can find a term like "basal body temperature," which is unfamiliar to most people—an expression referring to the temperature when the body is at rest.

Then, if bilingual dictionaries are so useful, why did my aunt give me a monolingual dictionary? As I found out, there is, in fact, often no perfect equivalence between words in one language and those in another. My aunt even goes so far as to claim that a Japanese "equivalent" can ever give you the real meaning of a word in

English! Therefore she insisted that I read the definition of a word in a monolingual dictionary when I wanted to obtain a better understanding of its meaning. Gradually, I have come to see what she meant.

Using a monolingual dictionary for learners has benefited me in another important way—my passive vocabulary (words I can understand) has increasingly become an active vocabulary (words I actually use). This dictionary uses a limited number of words, around 2,000, in its definitions. When I read these definitions, I am repeatedly exposed to basic words and how they are used to explain objects and concepts. Because of this, I can express myself more easily in English.

Once I got used to the monolingual dictionary for learners, I discovered another kind of monolingual dictionary, which is particularly useful when writing essays or preparing presentations. This is what can be called a "find-the-right-word"

37. Monolingual Dictionary

dictionary. This kind of dictionary enables me to come up with an alternative, and sometimes more precise, expression for a word I am already familiar with. For example, if I look up "difficult," I will find a group of related terms such as "challenging," "tough," "hard," and "demanding." A word like "important" will lead me to "significant," "crucial," "essential," "influential," and "major."

What I realize now is that both monolingual and bilingual dictionaries have particular uses, and your choice of dictionary depends on your aims. If you wish to understand the general meaning of texts in a foreign language and have no need to express your own ideas in the language, you may find a bilingual dictionary sufficient. If you work as a professional translator, you will find it necessary to use specialized bilingual dictionaries. However, if your ultimate goals are to understand a foreign language clearly and to speak or write the language using a variety of words, I strongly recommend that you obtain a monolingual dictionary once you have command of a basic vocabulary. I feel I owe the progress I have made in English to the wisdom of my aunt.

38. IT Revolution

My niece, Ann, is in her third year at university. She has recently started her job search. When she entered the university, she wanted to be an architect and planned to apply for work in an architectural firm. But as she prepared for her job search, she learned that the way people work has changed a lot in the last few years. She discovered that much of the change has occurred because of what is called the IT Revolution. The "IT (Information Technology) Revolution" refers to the dramatic change in the way information is perceived and used in today's world.

Over the past 12 to 15 years, the amount and types of data available on the Internet and, in particular, the speed at which we can process the data, have increased to an extent few people could have imagined. These developments have led to new ways of thinking about how we use information and how we work in information-rich environments. Simply put, doing business no longer relies on location; new information-sharing software has made cooperation at a distance convenient and efficient.

As a result, many new business models have appeared. One such model is a large corporation arranging to have another company, often located in a different country, perform essential tasks. This became possible with the growth of reliable and secure communications and the ability to move massive amounts of data over long distances in an instant. An early example of this arrangement is in the field of accounting. A company in the United States, for instance, first scans all its bills, orders, and wage payments into the computer and sends the documents to an accounting center in, say, Costa Rica. Basic

38. IT Revolution

accounting activity is then carried out at that site. Next, the data is returned via the Internet to the original company, where high-level analysis is done.

Another example of this type of arrangement is reliance on overseas call centers, which have become increasingly common. It has become possible for a telephone operator in India to answer a customer-service call from anywhere in the world, respond directly to the customer and offer a satisfactory solution, at a far lower cost to the company than ever before. Many large companies now depend on such call centers. Today in Japan, when you call a toll-free number, there is a chance that someone in Chingtao, China will answer the phone in Japanese to help solve your problem.

A second business model made possible by the IT Revolution is one in which work is divided into smaller, more specific tasks performed by individuals in different geographical locations. For example, freelance specialists who may be living at a great distance from each other can work together to produce a new semiconductor design. A member of the group living in California does some initial work on the project and uploads the result onto a server. A colleague in Japan spends the day making further additions to the design. Next, someone in Israel accesses it and does his/her portion of the job. Finally the group member in California downloads it and gives it a final check. Thus, freelance specialists in different parts of the world collaborate to complete a single project.

A similar example is that of a commercial artist who works in the privacy of her beachside home in Hawaii to create a mail-order catalog for a client in Paris. She uses pictures taken by a photographer in Australia, adds text composed by a writer in Canada, includes artwork she created

38. IT Revolution

on her computer, and sends the finished product out to the client for final approval. All this is done digitally and according to each worker's own schedule. In this way, the best talent in the world can be chosen for each task.

With the knowledge she has acquired in the course of her job search, Ann now understands how the nature of work has changed as a result of the IT Revolution. Although she is still interested in architecture, Ann now realizes that this field offers a broader variety of opportunities. Rather than studying architectural design itself, Ann has decided to become an expert in the specifications and materials that architects need for their designs. She also now knows that there is often not enough work in one office for a specialist of this type. However, she is confident she can work as a freelance specialist in collaboration with a variety of people in different countries. Ann now looks forward to taking advantage of the career opportunities that the IT Revolution has opened up.

39. Snowflake

The white-haired old man was sitting in his favorite chair, holding a thick book and rubbing his tired eyes. When his nineteen-year-old granddaughter, Valerie, came into the room, he looked up and smiled. His eyes instantly brightened with happiness to see her.

"Hi, Grandpa. What are you reading?" she asked, pulling up a chair beside him.

"Oh, it's a book on the architecture of Spain. But I'm not really reading. Mostly I am just falling asleep over the pictures," he said, laughing. "Are you finished packing your bags yet?" he asked. The following morning Valerie and two of her friends were flying to Europe for a two-week holiday.

"Almost. I need to travel light, you see, so I

can buy lots of new dresses and shoes in Paris and Barcelona." They both laughed because Valerie was not actually interested in fashion at all. She loved foreign languages, music, art, good food, and many other things—but not shopping for clothes.

"Have the three of you finally decided what you want to do on your trip?"

Valerie thought for a moment and then replied, "Well, Naomi really wants to see the Eiffel Tower and we all want to visit the Louvre Museum. Mika and I want to see the wonderful buildings in Barcelona, too. But, basically, we still don't have much of a plan. Do you have any suggestions? You've been to Europe so many times."

Valerie's grandfather paused, and then replied slowly, "You know, sometimes it may be best not to have a detailed plan. I remember when your grandmother and I first went to Barcelona. We went to museums or concerts every day. We saw

39. Snowflake

bullfights and soccer matches. We ate wonderful food and met many interesting people. But one of my greatest memories from that trip was completely unexpected." Grandpa paused again, and then said, "We had come especially to see the famous works of art, but one day just for a change we went to the zoo. And there I met someone who had a great effect on me."

"His name was Snowflake," he continued, "and he was a gorilla, a very special albino gorilla, with white fur and pink skin. When only three years old, Snowflake was captured in the forests of Africa and then brought to the zoo. Because of his rare color he had become quite famous. Many people lined up to see him behind a glass wall in the exhibit hall."

"In fact," Grandpa said, "I did not think he was real when I first saw him. When I moved closer, though, he turned slowly toward me and calmly looked directly into my eyes. For the first time ever, I felt intelligence and awareness in the eyes of another species. It made an impression on me that I will never forget."

"So, what did you do?" Valerie asked.

"Actually, Snowflake was the one who did something. As we gazed into each other's eyes, the 140-kilogram gorilla suddenly slapped his hand flat against the glass wall, making a loud, forceful sound that made all the people in the room cry out in surprise. Snowflake seemed rather pleased with our reaction, turning away casually and snacking on some leaves."

"So, he surprised you. He had a sense of humor, it seems," Valerie said. "But isn't it sad for such a wonderful animal to live in a cage?"

"Yes, maybe," Grandpa replied. "But in the wild so many gorillas are killed by hunters or disease that it is difficult to say which way of life is better. And Snowflake did live a long life for a gorilla, about forty years, which is equivalent to

39. Snowflake

eighty years for a human."

"So, he's dead now?" Valerie asked.

"Yes, he died of skin cancer in 2003. He had very pale skin, of course, so sunlight was very dangerous for him. It was a painful end, but I believe he had some happy memories, too. You know, he had three mates, several 'children,' and 22 'grandchildren,' so that must have been nice."

Grandpa smiled at Valerie and said, "Anyway, maybe it's best not to plan everything. All kinds of wonderful, unexpected encounters may be waiting for you on your trip."

A week or so later, Grandpa heard from Valerie and her friends. They were having a wonderful time, enjoying many new activities. They even made an unscheduled trip to the Barcelona Zoo, where they saw one of Snowflake's grandchildren. This baby gorilla didn't have white fur, but he did have bright, intelligent eyes which Valerie said she would never forget.

40. My Camp Memory

During my college days, I spent my summers as an assistant at a camp for junior high school students. It was work I looked forward to every year because it was a pleasure. Of my camp memories, there is one summer that stands out from the rest.

It was the first day of camp. About an hour after everyone had arrived, I noticed a small boy sitting alone under a tree. He was thin, pale and obviously uneasy. Only fifty feet away, all the other campers were playing, joking and enjoying getting to know each other, but he seemed to want to be anywhere other than where he was. He had a lost look, a look of deep loneliness. To be honest, I felt uncomfortable approaching him, but our senior staff members had instructed

40. MY CAMP MEMORY

us to watch for campers who might feel left out, campers just like this boy. I knew it was my responsibility to talk with him even though I felt it would not be easy.

I walked up to him and said, "Hi, my name is Kevin, and I'm one of the assistants." In a small, shaky voice he shyly answered, "Hi, I'm Tommy."

"Welcome to camp, Tommy. How's it going?"

"Okay, I guess," he said quietly, not looking at me.

"Do you want to join the activities and meet some new kids, or do you want to just sit here under this tree?" I asked with a smile. He replied unwillingly, "I'm fine here. This camp is not really my thing." It was clear that camp life was new to him, and I somehow knew it would not be right to push him to join the other campers. Instead, I sat down and talked with him for a while, and then took him to his cabin. I hoped he would make some friends there.

After lunch the next day, I led the two hundred campers in songs. I looked over the enthusiastic crowd and noticed Tommy, sitting alone, staring at the floor. I realized he was going to require some very special care. That night at our staff meeting, I told everyone about him, and asked them to pay attention to him and spend time with him whenever possible. Tommy became our special project. We always helped him participate in the camp activities, and slowly he opened up.

Time passed quickly, and Tommy became more active every day. In no time camp was over. As the campers celebrated at a farewell party, I suddenly saw what would be one of the most vivid memories of my life. The boy who had once sat alone under the tree was now dancing. Towards the end of the party, he was dancing as if he owned the dance floor, and talking with

40. My Camp Memory

people he had not even been able to look at a few weeks earlier. The changes in Tommy were dramatic. All of the camp staff saw him as the camp's greatest success.

About five years later, I got a letter from Tommy. I had not seen him since the night he was all over the dance floor, so it was a complete surprise to get a letter from him. And what the letter said was even more of a surprise.

In the letter, Tommy said, "I appreciate your help very much. On the first day of camp, you came up to me while I was sitting alone. After that, you always gave me special attention and encouraged me to join activities when I hesitated. As a result, I gradually got to know the other campers, and I even became 'the king of the dance floor' on the last night. Because of your help that summer, my life changed. I gained so much confidence that I went back to school as a new person. My grades improved. I became very active and made new friends. Today, I got a letter that said I have been given a scholarship for college next year. I am proud to have gotten it, but I know that if you had not helped me, I would not have. I just wanted to thank you for helping me become a different person."

I have kept that letter; it is special to me. I read it sometimes to remind myself that we never know how much our actions may affect someone.

41. The Rocks

Going to the shore on the first morning of the vacation, Jerry stopped and looked at a wild and rocky bay, and then over to the crowded beach he knew so well from other years. His mother looked back at him.

"Are you tired of the usual beach, Jerry?"

"Oh, no!" he said quickly, but then said, "I'd like to look at those rocks down there."

"Of course, if you like."

Jerry watched his mother go, then ran straight into the water and began swimming. He was a good swimmer. He swam out over the gleaming sand and then he was in the real sea.

He saw some older, local boys—men, to him—sitting on the rocks. One smiled and waved. It was enough to make him feel welcome.

In a minute, he had swum over and was on the rocks beside them. Then, as he watched, the biggest of the boys dived into the water, and did not come up. Jerry gave a cry of alarm, but after a long time the boy came up on the other side of a big dark rock, letting out a shout of victory. Immediately the rest of them dived and Jerry was alone. He counted the seconds they were under water: one, two, three . . . fifty . . . one hundred. At one hundred and sixty, one then another, of the boys came up on the far side of the rock and Jerry understood that they had swum through some gap or hole in it. He knew then that he wanted to be like them. He watched as they swam away and then swam to shore himself.

Next day he swam back to the rocks. There was nobody else there. He looked at the great rock the boys had swum through. He could see no gap in it. He dived down to its base, again and again. It took a long time, but finally, while he

41. The Rocks

was holding on to the base of the rock, he shot his feet out forward and they met no obstacle. He had found the hole.

In the days that followed, Jerry hurried to the rocks every morning and exercised his lungs as if everything, the whole of his life, depended on it. He counted how long he could hold his breath. Each day he improved his time. Even back at home he timed himself by the clock, and was proud to find he could hold his breath for two minutes. The authority of the clock brought close the adventure that was so important to him.

The day after tomorrow, his mother reminded him casually one morning, they must go home. He swam straight out to the rock and looked down into the water. This was the moment when he would try. If he did not do it now, he never would. He filled his lungs, started to count, and dived to the bottom.

He was soon inside the dark, narrow hole.

The water pushed him up against the roof. The roof was sharp and hurt his back. He pulled himself along with his hands—fast, fast. His head knocked against something; a sharp pain dizzied him. he counted: one hundred . . . one hundred and fifteen. The hole had widened! He gave himself a kick forward and swam as fast as he could. He lost track of time and said one hundred and fifteen to himself again. Then he saw light. Victory filled him. His hands, reaching forward, met nothing; and his feet propelled him out into the open sea. He floated to the surface, pulled himself up onto the rock and lay face down, catching his breath. After a time he felt better and sat up. Then he swam to shore and climbed slowly up the path to the house.

His mother came to meet him, smiling.

"Have a nice time?" she asked.

"Oh, yes, thank you," he said.

"How did you cut your head?"

41. The Rocks

"Oh, I just cut it."

They sat down to lunch together.

"Mom," he said, "I can hold my breath for two minutes—three minutes."

"Can you, darling?" she said. "Well, you shouldn't overdo it. You look a bit pale. I don't think you ought to swim any more today."

She was ready for a battle of wills, but he gave in at once. It was no longer of the least importance to go to the bay.

Word List

- 本文で使われている全ての語を掲載しています。
- 語形が規則変化する語の見出しは原形で示しています。不規則変化語は本文中で使われている形になっています。
- 一般的な意味を紹介していますので、一部の語で本文で実際に使われている品詞や意味と合っていないことがあります。
- 品詞は以下のように示しています

名 名詞	代 代名詞	形 形容詞	副 副詞	動 動詞	助 助動詞
前 前置詞	接 接続詞	間 間投詞	冠 冠詞	略 略語	俗 俗語
熟 熟語	頭 接頭語	尾 接尾語	号 記号	関 関係代名詞	

A

- **a** 冠 ①1つの、1人の、ある ②〜につき
- **ability** 名 ①できること、(〜する)能力 ②才能
- **able** 形 ①《be - to 〜》(人が)〜することができる ②能力のある
- **about** 副 ①およそ、約 ②まわりに、あたりを 前 ①〜について ②〜のまわりに[の] How about 〜? 〜はどうですか。〜しませんか。 What about 〜? 〜についてあなたはどう思いますか。〜はどうですか。 be about to まさに〜しようとしている、〜するところだ
- **above** 前 ①〜の上に ②〜より上で、〜以上で ③〜を超えて 副 ①上に ②以上に 形 上記の 名《the - 》上記の人[こと]
- **abroad** 副 海外で[に] go abroad 外国へ行く
- **absolutely** 副 ①完全に、確実に ②《yesを強調する返事として》そうですとも
- **academy** 名 ①アカデミー、学士院 ②学園、学院
- **accept** 動 ①受け入れる ②同意する、認める
- **access** 名 ①接近、近づく方法、通路 ②(システムなどへの)アクセス 動 アクセスする
- **accident** 名 ①(不慮の)事故、災難 ②偶然 by accident 偶然に
- **accidentally** 副 偶然に、誤って
- **according** 副《- to 〜》〜によれば[よると]
- **account** 名 ①計算書 ②勘定、預金口座 ③報告、説明、記述 take into account 〜を考慮に入れる 動 ①《- for 〜》〜を説明する、〜(の割合)を占める、〜の原因となる ②〜を…とみなす
- **accounting** 名 会計、経理
- **achieve** 動 成し遂げる、達成する、成功を収める
- **acquire** 動 ①(努力して)獲得する、確保する ②(学力、技術などを)習得する
- **across** 前 〜を渡って、〜の向こう側に、(身体の一部に)かけて 副 渡って、向こう側に come across ふと出会う[見つける]
- **action** 名 ①行動、活動 ②動作、行為 ③機能、作用
- **active** 形 ①活動的な ②積極的な ③活動[作動]中の active

vocabulary 使用語彙 take an active role 積極的な役割を担う

- **activity** 名 活動, 活気 physical activity 身体活動
- **actually** 副 実際に, 本当に, 実は
- **add** 動 ①加える, 足す ②足し算をする ③言い添える
- **added** 形 追加された
- **addition** 名 ①付加, 追加, 添加 ②足し算 in addition 加えて, さらに in addition to ~に加えて
- **additionally** 副 さらに, その上
- **address** 名 ①住所, アドレス ②演説 動 ①あて名を書く ②演説をする, 話しかける
- **adjust** 動 ①適応する[させる], 慣れる ②調整する ③(意見の食い違い・論争などを)解決する, 調停する ④(間違いなどを)訂正する
- **adjustment** 名 ①調整, 調節 ②適応 ③調停
- **administrator** 名 経営者, 理事, 管理者
- **admiration** 名 賞賛(の的), 感嘆
- **admire** 動 感心する, 賞賛する
- **adolescence** 名 青春期
- **adolescent** 形 青春期の, 若々しい
- **adult** 名 大人, 成人 形 大人の, 成人した
- **adulthood** 名 成人期
- **advanced** 動 advance(進む)の過去, 過去分詞 形 上級の, 先に進んだ, 高等の
- **advantage** 名 有利な点[立場], 強み, 優越 take advantage of ~を利用する, ~につけ込む
- **adventure** 名 冒険 動 危険をおかす
- **advertise** 動 ①広告する, 宣伝する ②告知する
- **advice** 名 忠告, 助言, 意見

- **advise** 動 忠告する, 勧める 《be》advised to ~するよう忠告される
- **aerobic** 名 エアロビクス 形 エアロビクスの
- **affect** 動 ①影響する ②(病気などが)おかす ③ふりをする 名 感情, 欲望
- **afraid** 形 ①心配して ②恐れて, こわがって I'm afraid (that) 残念ながら~, 悪いけれど~
- **Africa** 名 アフリカ《大陸》
- **African-American** 名 アフリカ系アメリカ人 形 アフリカ系アメリカ人の
- **Afro-American** 名 アフリカ系アメリカ人 形 アフリカ系アメリカ人の
- **after** 前 ①~の後に[で], ~の次に ②《前後に名詞がきて》次々に~, 何度も~《反復・継続を表す》after all 結局 After you. どうぞお先に. one after another 次々に 副 後に[で] 接 (~した)後に[で]
- **afterward** 副 その後, のちに
- **again** 副 再び, もう一度
- **against** 前 ①~に対して, ~に反対して, (規則など)に違反して ②~にもたれて
- **age** 名 ①年齢 ②時代, 年代
- **aged** 形 ①年を取った ②《the -》年寄りたち, 老人
- **ago** 副 ~前に
- **agree** 動 ①同意する ②意見が一致する
- **ahead** 副 ①前方へ[に] ②前もって ③進歩して, 有利に ahead of ~より先[前]に, ~に先んじて speed ahead 加速前進して
- **aim** 動 ①(武器・カメラなどを)向ける ②ねらう, 目指す 名 ねらい, 目標
- **air** 名 ①《the -》空中, 空間 ②空気, 《the -》大気 ③雰囲気, 様子 air pollution 大気汚染

- □ **airplane** 名 飛行機
- □ **Akihabara** 名 秋葉原《地名》
- □ **alarm** 名 ①警報, 目覚まし時計 ②驚き, 突然の恐怖 動 ①はっとさせる ②警報を発する
- □ **albino** 名 アルビノ
- □ **alcohol** 名 アルコール
- □ **all** 形 すべての, ~中 代 全部, すべて(のもの[人]) not ~ at all 少しも[全然]~ない if at all 仮にあったとしても 名 全体 副 まったく, すっかり all right よろしい, 申し分ない, わかった, 承知した
- □ **allergen** 名 アレルゲン, アレルギー誘発物質
- □ **allergy** 名 アレルギー
- □ **allergy-causing** 形 アレルギーを誘発する
- □ **allow** 動 ①許す, 《- … to ~》…が~するのを可能にする, …に~させておく ②与える
- □ **almost** 副 ほとんど, もう少しで(~するところ)
- □ **alone** 形 ただひとりの 副 ひとりで, ~だけで leave ~ alone ~をそっとしておく
- □ **along** 前 ~に沿って 副 前へ, ずっと, 進んで get along with (人)と仲良くする
- □ **alongside** 副 そばに, 並んで 前 ~のそばに, ~と並んで
- □ **alphabet** 名 ①アルファベット, 文字, 文字体系 ②初歩
- □ **already** 副 すでに, もう
- □ **also** 副 ~も(また), ~も同様に not only A but also B Aだけでなく B も 接 その上, さらに
- □ **alter** 動 (部分的に)変える, 変わる
- □ **alternative** 形 代わりの, 代替の 名 2つのうちの1つ, 代替え手段, 代替案
- □ **although** 接 ~だけれども, ~にもかかわらず, たとえ~でも
- □ **always** 副 いつも, 常に not always 必ずしも~であるとは限らない
- □ **am** 動 ~である, (~に)いる[ある]《主語がIのときのbeの現在形》
- □ **amazed** 動 amaze (びっくりさせる)の過去, 過去分詞 形 びっくりした, 驚いた
- □ **amazing** 動 amaze (びっくりさせる)の現在分詞 形 驚くべき, 見事な
- □ **Amazon** 名 ①《the -》アマゾン川 ②アマゾン族《ギリシア神話に出てくる勇猛な女族》
- □ **ambition** 名 大望, 野心
- □ **America** 名 アメリカ《国名・大陸》
- □ **American** 形 アメリカ(人)の 名 アメリカ人
- □ **among** 前 (3つ以上のもの)の間で[に], ~の中で[に]
- □ **amount** 名 ①量, 額 ②《the -》合計 動 (総計~に)なる
- □ **Amy** 名 エイミー《人名》
- □ **an** 冠 ①1つの, 1人の, ある ②~につき
- □ **analysis** 名 分析, 解析(学)
- □ **ancient** 形 昔の, 古代の ancient civilization 古代文明
- □ **and** 接 ①そして, ~と… ②《同じ語を結んで》ますます ③《結果を表して》それで, だから and so on ~など
- □ **Andy** 名 アンディ《人名》
- □ **Angela** 名 アンジェラ《人名》
- □ **anger** 名 怒り
- □ **angrily** 副 怒って, 腹立たしげに
- □ **angry** 形 怒って, 腹を立てて
- □ **animal** 名 動物 形 動物の animal track 動物の足跡
- □ **anime** 名 (日本製)アニメ
- □ **Ann** 名 アン《人名》
- □ **Anna** 名 アンナ《人名》

Word List

- **announce** 動(人に)知らせる、公表する
- **announcement** 名発表、アナウンス、告示、声明
- **annual** 形年1回の、例年の、年次の 名①年報 ②一年生植物
- **another** 形①もう1つ[1人]の ②別の 代①もう1つ[1人] ②別のもの　one another お互いに
- **answer** 動①答える、応じる ②《- for ~》~の責任を負う 名答え、応答、返事
- **anxious** 形①心配な、不安な ②切望して
- **any** 形①《疑問文で》何か、いくつかの ②《否定文で》何も、少しも(~ない) ③《肯定文で》どの~も 代①《疑問文で》(~のうち)何か、どれか、誰か ②《否定文で》少しも、何も[誰も]~ない ③《肯定文で》どれも、誰でも　if any もしあれば、あったとしても 副少しは、少しも
- **anyone** 代①《疑問文・条件節で》誰か ②《否定文で》誰も(~ない) ③《肯定文で》誰でも
- **anything** 代①《疑問文で》何か、どれでも ②《否定文で》何も、どれも(~ない) ③《肯定文で》何でも、どれでも　anything but 何でも、少しも~でない 副いくらか
- **anyway** 副①いずれにせよ、ともかく ②どんな方法でも
- **anywhere** 副どこかへ[に]、どこにも、どこへも、どこにでも
- **apart** 副①ばらばらに、離れて ②別にして、それだけで　apart from ~ から離れて
- **apartment** 名アパート
- **appeal** 動①求める、訴える ②(人の)気に入る 名①要求、訴え ②魅力、人気
- **appealing** 形魅力的な
- **appear** 動①現れる、見えてくる ②(~のように)見える、~らしい

appear to するように見える

- **appearance** 名①現れること、出現 ②外見、印象
- **apple** 名リンゴ
- **apply** 動①申し込む、志願する ②あてはまる ③適用する
- **appreciate** 動①正しく評価する、よさがわかる ②価値[相場]が上がる ③ありがたく思う
- **approach** 動①接近する ②話を持ちかける 名接近、(~へ)近づく道
- **appropriate** 形①適切な、ふさわしい、妥当な ②特殊な、特有の 動①割り当てる ②自分のものにする、占有する
- **approval** 名①賛成 ②承認、認可
- **approximately** 副おおよそ、だいたい
- **architect** 名建築家、設計者 動設計する
- **architectural** 形建築上の
- **architecture** 名①建築(学)、建築物(様式) ②構成、構造　modern architecture 現代建築
- **are** 動~である、(~に)いる[ある]《主語がyou, we, theyまたは複数名詞のときのbeの現在形》名アール《面積単位、100平方メートル》
- **area** 名①地域、地方、区域、場所 ②面積
- **argue** 動①論じる、議論する ②主張する
- **Ariès** 名フィリップ・アリエス《フランスの中世社会研究を主とする歴史家、1914-1984》
- **around** 副①まわりに、あちこちに ②およそ、約　get around 広まる 前~のまわりに、~のあちこちに
- **arrange** 動①並べる、整える ②取り決める ③準備する、手はずを整える
- **arrangement** 名①準備、手配 ②取り決め、協定 ③整頓、配置

- **arrival** 名①到着 ②到達
- **arrive** 動到着する,到達する
- **art** 名芸術,美術
- **article** 名①(法令・誓約などの)箇条,項目 ②(新聞・雑誌などの)記事,論文
- **artist** 名芸術家
- **artwork** 名アートワーク,芸術作品
- **as** 接①《as ~ as …の形で》…と同じくらい ②~のとおりに,~のように ③~しながら,~しているときに ④~するにつれて,~にしたがって ⑤~なので ⑥~だけれども ⑦~する限りでは **as ~ as one can** できる限り~ **as a result** 結果として **as a whole** 概して,総じて **as for** ~はどうかというと,~に関しては **as if [though]** まるで~のように **as to** ~については,~に応じて **so as to** ~するために **so far as** ~する限り 前①~として(の) ②~の時 副同じくらい 代①~のような ②~だが
- **ashamed** 形恥じた,気が引けた,《be - of ~》~が恥ずかしい,~を恥じている
- **Asia** 名アジア
- **aside** 副わきへ(に),離れて **set aside** 取っておく,確保する
- **ask** 動①尋ねる,聞く ②頼む,求める **ask for** ~を求める
- **asleep** 形①眠って(いる状態の) ②(手足が)しびれている 副①眠って,休止して ②(手足が)しびれて **fall asleep** 眠り込む,寝入る
- **aspect** 名①状況,局面,側面 ②外観,様子 **negative aspect** マイナスの側面
- **assign** 動任命する,割り当てる 名譲り受け人
- **assigned** 形割り当てられた
- **assignment** 名①仕事,任務,宿題 ②割り当て

- **assistant** 名助手,補佐,店員 形援助の,補佐の
- **associated** 形結びついた,関連した 《be》 **associated with** ~と関連する
- **association** 名①交際,連合,結合 ②連想 ③協会,組合
- **astronaut** 名宇宙飛行士
- **at** 前①《場所・時》~に[で] ②《目標・方向》~に[を],~に向かって ③《原因・理由》~を見て[聞いて・知って] ④~に従事して,~の状態で
- **ATC** 略 air traffic controller 航空管制官
- **ate** 動 eat (食べる)の過去
- **atmosphere** 名①大気,空気 ②雰囲気
- **attempt** 動試みる,企てる **attempt the tricks** わざを試す 名試み,企て,努力
- **attention** 名①注意,集中 ②配慮,手当て,世話 間《号令として》気をつけ
- **attitude** 名姿勢,態度,心構え
- **attraction** 名引きつけるもの,出し物,アトラクション
- **attractive** 形魅力的な,あいきょうのある
- **attractiveness** 名人を引きつけること
- **aunt** 名おば
- **Australia** 名オーストラリア《国名》
- **authority** 名①権威,権力,権限 ②《the -ties》(関係)当局
- **availability** 名①利用できること,入手できるもの ②有益,有用性
- **available** 形利用[使用・入手]できる,得られる
- **avenue** 名①並木道 ②《A-, Ave.》~通り,~街
- **average** 名平均(値),並み **on (the) average** 平均して 形平均の,

Word List

普通の 動平均して~になる
- □ **avoid** 動避ける, (~を)しないようにする
- □ **awareness** 名認識, 自覚, 意識性, 気づいていること
- □ **away** 副離れて, 遠くに, 去って, わきに 形離れた, 遠征した 名遠征試合
- □ **awful** 形①ひどい, 不愉快な ②恐ろしい 副ひどく, とても
- □ **Axelrod** 名《Lake -》アクセルロッド湖

B

- □ **baby** 名①赤ん坊 ②《呼びかけで》あなた 形①赤ん坊の ②小さな
- □ **back** 名①背中 ②裏, 後ろ 副①戻って ②後ろへ[に] on the way back 帰り道の途中で 形裏の, 後ろの
- □ **background** 名背景, 前歴, 生い立ち
- □ **backpack** 名バックパック, リュックサック
- □ **backstage** 副舞台裏[袖]で, 楽屋で 形舞台[楽屋]裏の 名舞台裏, 楽屋
- □ **bacteria** 名バクテリア, 細菌
- □ **bad** 形①悪い, へたな, まずい ②気の毒な ③(程度が)ひどい, 激しい in a bad way 悪い方向に
- □ **bag** 名袋, かばん 動袋に入れる, つかまえる
- □ **balance** 名①均衡, 平均, 落ち着き ②てんびん ③残高, 差額 動釣り合いをとる
- □ **ball** 名ボール, 球 rice ball おにぎり 動丸くなる, 丸める
- □ **balsamic vinegar** バルサミコ酢
- □ **bandage** 名包帯, 巻き布 動包帯をする
- □ **barbecue** 名バーベキュー 動丸焼きする, あぶって焼く
- □ **Barcelona** 名バルセロナ《スペインの都市》
- □ **bare** 形裸の, むき出しの 動裸にする, むき出しにする
- □ **barrier** 名さく, 防壁, 障害(物), 障壁 動防壁で囲む
- □ **basal** 形基礎の, 基本的な basal body temperature 基礎体温
- □ **base** 名基礎, 土台, 本部 動《 - on ~》~に基礎を置く, 基づく
- □ **-based** 形~をベース[基礎]にした
- □ **basement** 名地下(室), 基部
- □ **basic** 形基礎の, 基本の command of a basic vocabulary 基礎語彙力 名《-s》基礎, 基本, 必需品
- □ **basically** 副基本的には, 大筋では
- □ **basis** 名①土台, 基礎 ②基準, 原理 ③根拠 ④主成分
- □ **bath** 名入浴, 水浴, 風呂 動入浴[水浴]する[させる]
- □ **bathe** 動①水浴する, 水浴びする ②風呂に入る[入れる] ③傷口を洗う
- □ **battle** 名戦闘, 戦い battle of wills 意地の張り合い 動戦う
- □ **bay** 名湾, 入り江
- □ **be** 動~である, (~に)いる[ある], ~となる 助①《現在分詞とともに用いて》~している ②《過去分詞とともに用いて》~される, ~されている
- □ **beach** 名海辺, 浜
- □ **beachside** 名浜辺の
- □ **bean** 名豆
- □ **bear** 動①運ぶ ②支える ③耐える ④(子を)産む 名①熊 ②(株取引で)弱気
- □ **beautiful** 形美しい, すばらしい 間いいぞ, すばらしい
- □ **beauty** 名①美, 美しい人[物] ②

《the -》美点

- **became** 動 become (なる) の過去
- **because** 接 (なぜなら)〜だから, 〜という理由[原因]で because of 〜のために, 〜の理由で
- **become** 動 ①(〜に)なる ②(〜に)似合う ③become の過去分詞
- **bedcover** 名 ベッドカバー
- **been** 動 be (〜である) の過去分詞 動 be (〜している・〜される) の過去分詞
- **before** 前 〜の前に[で], 〜より以前 接 〜する前に 副 以前に
- **began** 動 begin (始まる) の過去
- **begin** 動 始まる[始める], 起こる
- **beginning** 動 begin (始まる) の現在分詞 名 初め, 始まり
- **behavior** 名 振る舞い, 態度, 行動 improper behavior 不適切な行為
- **behind** 前 ①〜の後ろに, 〜の背後に ②〜に遅れて, 〜に劣って 副 ①後ろに, 背後に ②遅れて, 劣って leave behind あとにする
- **belief** 名 信じること, 信念, 信用
- **believe** 動 信じる, 信じている, (〜と)思う, 考える believe it or not まさかと思うでしょうが
- **belong** 動《- to 〜》〜に属する, 〜のものである
- **below** 前 ①〜より下に ②〜以下の, 〜より劣る 副 下に[へ]
- **benefit** 名 ①利益, 恩恵 ②(失業保険・年金などの)手当, 給付(金) 動 利益を得る, (〜の)ためになる
- **Benjamin Franklin** ベンジャミン・フランクリン《米国の政治家・発明家, 1706-1790》
- **beside** 前 ①〜のそばに, 〜と並んで ②〜と比べると ③〜とはずれて
- **besides** 前 ①〜に加えて, 〜のほかに ②《否定文・疑問文で》〜を除いて 副 その上, さらに
- **best** 形 最もよい, 最大[多]の 副 最もよく, 最も上手に best of all 何よりも, いちばん 名《the -》①最上のもの ②全力, 精いっぱい at one's best 最高の状態で at (the) best せいぜい, よくても do[try] one's best 全力を尽くす
- **better** 形 ①よりよい ②(人が)回復して 副 ①よりよく, より上手に ②むしろ had better 〜するほうがよい, 〜しなさい
- **between** 前 (2つのもの)の間に[で・の] 副 間に
- **big** 形 ①大きい ②偉い, 重要な 副 ①大きく, 大いに ②自慢して
- **bilingual** 形 バイリンガルの, 2言語を使いこなす 名 2言語に通じた人
- **bill** 名 ①請求書, 勘定書 ②法案 ③紙幣 ④ビラ ⑤くちばし 動 ①請求書を送る ②勘定書に記入する
- **biological** 形 ①生物学(上)の, 生物学的な ②血のつながった
- **bird** 名 鳥
- **birthday** 名 誕生日
- **bit** 動 bite (かむ) の過去, 過去分詞 名 ①小片, 少量 ②《a -》少し, ちょっと ③(情報量単位の)ビット quite a bit 相当に
- **bite** 動 かむ, かじる 名 かむこと, かみ傷, ひと口 insect bites 虫刺されのあと
- **bitten** 動 bite (かむ) の過去分詞 get bitten (虫に)さされる
- **black** 形 黒い, 有色の 名 黒, 黒色
- **blame** 動 とがめる, 非難する 名 ①責任, 罪 ②非難
- **blanket** 名 毛布 動 毛布でくるむ
- **block** 名 ①(市街地の)1区画 ②大きな固まり, ブロック 動 妨げる, ふさぐ
- **blood** 名 ①血, 血液 ②血統, 家柄 ③気質 high blood pressure 高血圧症
- **blouse** 名 ブラウス, 上着

WORD LIST

- **blue** 形 ①青い ②青ざめた ③憂うつな、陰気な 名 青(色)
- **Blue Hills** ブルーヒルズ《地名》
- **Bobby** 名 ボビー《人名》
- **body** 名 ①体、死体、胴体 ②団体、組織 ③主要部、(文書の)本文
- **bone** 名 ①骨、《-s》骨格 ②《-s》要点、骨組み 動 (魚・肉)の骨をとる
- **book** 名 ①本、書物 ②《the B-》聖書 ③《-s》帳簿 動 ①記入する、記帳する ②予約する
- **bookshelf** 名 本棚
- **born** 動 bear (産む)の過去分詞 《be》**born into** ~に生まれる 形 生まれた、生まれながらの
- **boss** 名 上司、親方、監督
- **both** 形 両方の、2つとも 副《both ~ and … の形で》~も…も両方とも 代 両方、両者、双方
- **bother** 動 悩ます、困惑させる 名 面倒、いざこざ、悩みの種
- **bottom** 名 ①底、下部、すそ野、ふもと、最下位、根底 ②尻 形 底の、根底の
- **box** 名 ①箱、容器 ②観覧席 ③詰所 動 ①箱に入れる[詰める] ②ボクシングをする
- **boy** 名 ①少年、男の子 ②給仕
- **brand-new** 形 新品の、真新しい
- **brave** 形 勇敢な 動 勇敢に立ち向かう
- **Brazil** 名 ブラジル《国》
- **Brazilian** 形 ブラジル(人)の 名 ブラジル人
- **break** 動 ①壊す、折る ②(記録・法律・約束)を破る ③中断する **break into** ~に押し入る、急に~する **break out** 発生する、急に起こる **break up** ばらばらになる、解散させる 名 ①破壊、割れ目 ②小休止 **Give me a break.** いいかげんにしろよ。
- **breakfast** 名 朝食

- **breath** 名 ①息、呼吸 ②《a-》(風の)そよぎ、気配、きざし
- **Brian** 名 ブライアン《人名》
- **bright** 形 ①輝いている、鮮明な ②快活な ③利口な 副 輝いて、明るく
- **brighten** 動 輝かせる、快活にさせる
- **brim** 名 (容器の)縁、(帽子の)つば 動 縁までいっぱいになる
- **bring** 動 ①持ってくる、連れてくる ②もたらす、生じる **bring about** 引き起こす **bring close** ~に近づける **bring forth** 生み出す **bring up** 育てる
- **Britain** 名 大ブリテン(島)
- **British** 形 ①英国人の ②イギリス英語の 名 英国人
- **broad** 形 ①幅の広い ②寛大な ③明白な 副 すっかり、十分に
- **broadcast** 名 放送、番組 動 放送する、広める 形 放送の
- **brother** 名 ①兄弟 ②同僚、同胞
- **brought** 動 bring (持ってくる)の過去、過去分詞
- **brush** 名 ①ブラシ ②絵筆 動 ブラシをかける、払いのける
- **bucket** 名 バケツ
- **build** 動 建てる、確立する **build up** 作り上げる、確立する 名 体格、構造
- **building** 動 build (建てる)の現在分詞 名 建物、建造物、ビルディング
- **bullfight** 名 闘牛
- **burn** 動 燃える、燃やす、日焼けする[させる] 名 やけど、日焼け
- **bus** 名 バス
- **bus stop** バス停
- **bush** 名 低木、やぶ、未開墾地
- **bushy** 形 茂みのような、毛がふさふさ[もじゃもじゃ]した
- **business** 名 ①職業、仕事 ②商売 ③用事 ④出来事、やっかいなこ

と **business model** ビジネスモデル 形 ①職業の ②商売上の
- **busy** 形 ①忙しい ②(電話で)話し中 ③にぎやかな, 交通が激しい
- **but** 接 ①でも, しかし ②~を除いて 前 ~を除いて, ~のほかは 副 ただ, のみ, ほんの
- **butterfly** 名 チョウ(蝶)
- **buy** 動 買う, 獲得する 名 購入, 買った[買える]物
- **by** 前 ①《位置》~のそばに[で] ②《手段・方法・行為者・基準》~によって, ~で ③《期限》~までには ④《通過・経由》~を経由して, ~を通って 副 そばに, 通り過ぎて

C

- **C** 略 Celsius 摂氏(の)
- **cabin** 名 (丸太作りの)小屋, 船室, キャビン
- **cafeteria** 名 カフェテリア, 社員食堂
- **cage** 名 鳥かご, 檻
- **calculate** 動 ①計算する, 算出する ②見積もる, 予想する
- **calendar** 名 カレンダー, 暦
- **California** 名 カリフォルニア《米国の州》
- **call** 動 ①呼ぶ, 叫ぶ ②電話をかける ③立ち寄る **call over** (人を)呼び寄せる, 招く ③《呼び声, 叫び ②(電話(をかけること) ③短い訪問
- **calm** 形 穏やかな, 落ち着いた 名 静けさ, 落ち着き 動 静まる, 鎮める
- **calmly** 副 落ち着いて, 静かに
- **calmness** 名 静けさ
- **calorie** 名 カロリー
- **came** 動 come (来る)の過去
- **camp** 名 ①野営(地), キャンプ ②収容所 動 野営する, キャンプする
- **camper** 名 キャンプする人
- **campground** 名 キャンプ場[地]
- **camping** 名 キャンプ生活, キャンプすること
- **can** 動 ①~できる ②~してもよい ③~でありうる ④《否定文で》~のはずがない **can ever give** (人)に与えられうる **Can I ~?** ~してもよいですか. **Can you ~?** ~してくれますか. 名 缶, 容器 動 缶詰[瓶詰]にする
- **Canada** 名 カナダ《国名》
- **cancer** 名 癌 **skin cancer** 皮膚がん
- **cane** 名 ①茎 ②(籐製の)杖 **sugar cane** サトウキビ
- **cannot** can (~できる)の否定形 (=can not)
- **capital** 名 ①首都 ②大文字 ③資本(金) 形 ①資本の ②首都の ③最も重要な ④大文字の
- **capture** 動 捕える 名 捕えること, 捕獲(物)
- **car** 名 自動車, (列車の)車両
- **carbonated** 形 炭酸を含む **carbonated drink** 炭酸飲料
- **card** 名 ①カード, 券, 名刺, はがき ②トランプ, 《-s》トランプ遊び
- **care** 名 心配, 注意 **take care** 気をつける, 注意する **take care of** ~の世話をする, ~に気をつける, ~を処理する 動 ①《通例否定文・疑問文で》気にする, 心配する ②世話をする **care for** ~の世話をする, ~に関心を持つ《否定文・疑問文で》~を好む
- **career** 名 ①(生涯の・専門的な)職業 ②経歴, キャリア
- **careful** 形 注意深い, 慎重な
- **carefully** 副 注意深く, 丹念に
- **caring** 形 世話をする, 思いやりのある
- **Carla** 名 カーラ《人名》
- **Carol** 名 キャロル《人名》

WORD LIST

- **carry** 動①運ぶ,連れていく,持ち歩く ②伝わる,伝える carry on ~を続ける carry out 実行する,成し遂げる
- **case** 名①事件,問題,事柄 ②実例,場合 ③実状,状況,症状 ④箱 in any case どんな場合でも,とにかく in case《接続詞的に》もし~である場合,万一~の場合 in case of ~の場合には,~に備えて
- **casually** 副何気なく,軽い気持ちで,偶然に
- **cat** 名ネコ(猫)
- **catalog** 名カタログ,目録
- **catch** 動①つかまえる ②追いつく ③(病気に)かかる catch up with ~に追いつく 名つかまえること,捕球
- **cater** 動提供する,満たす cater to (要求に)応じる,~を満たす
- **cattle** 名畜牛,家畜 cattle rancher 牛の牧場主
- **caught** 動 catch(つかまえる)の過去,過去分詞
- **cause** 名原因,理由,動機 動(~の)原因となる,引き起こす
- **celebrate** 動①祝う,祝福する ②祝典を開く
- **center** 名①中心,中央 ②中心地[人物] 動集中する[させる]
- **central** 形中央の,主要な central plaza セントラルプラザ
- **century** 名100年間,1世紀
- **ceremony** 名①儀式,式典 ②礼儀,作法,形式ばること
- **certain** 形①確実な,必ず~する ②(人が)確信した ③ある ④いくらかの 代(~の中の)いくつか
- **certainly** 副①確かに,必ず ②《返答に用いて》もちろん,そのとおり,承知しました
- **chair** 名①いす ②《the-》議長[会長]の席[職]

- **challenging** 動 challenge(挑戦する)の現在分詞 形能力が試される,やる気をそそる
- **championship** 名選手権(試合)
- **chance** 名①偶然,運 ②好機 ③見込み by any chance ひょっとして by chance 偶然 形偶然の,思いがけない 動偶然見つける
- **change** 動①変わる,変える ②交換する ③両替する 名①変化,変更 ②取り替え,乗り換え ③つり銭,小銭 for a change 気分転換に
- **channel** 名①チャンネル ②通路,水路,経路 ③海峡 動水路になる,道を開く
- **character** 名①特性,個性 ②(小説・劇などの)登場人物 ③文字,記号 ④品性,人格
- **characteristic** 形特徴のある,独特の 名特徴,特性,特色,持ち味
- **chart** 名表,図表,カルテ 動図で示す,図表にする pie chart 円グラフ
- **cheap** 形①(値段が)安い ②つまらない,質の悪い 副安っぽく
- **check** 動①照合する,検査する ②阻止[妨害]する ③(所持品を)預ける 名①照合,検査 ②小切手 ③(突然の)停止,阻止(するもの) ④伝票,勘定書
- **chemical** 形化学の,化学的な 名化学製品[薬品]
- **chew** 動①かむ ②じっくり考える 名かむこと,そしゃく
- **Chico Mendes** シコ・メンデス《ブラジルのゴム樹液採取者で環境保護活動家,1944–1988》
- **child** 名子ども
- **childhood** 名幼年[子ども]時代
- **childish** 形子どもっぽい,幼稚な
- **children** 名 child(子ども)の複数
- **Children's Day** 子どもの日
- **China** 名①中国《国名》②《c-》陶

磁器, 瀬戸物
- **Chingtao** 名 青島《中国山東省の都市》
- **Chizuko** 名 千津子《人名》
- **chocolate** 名 チョコレート
- **choice** 名 選択(の範囲・自由), えり好み, 選ばれた人[物] 形 精選した
- **choose** 動 選ぶ, (〜に)決める
- **chose** 動 choose (選ぶ)の過去
- **chosen** 動 choose (選ぶ)の過去分詞 形 選ばれた, 精選された
- **circle** 名 ①円, 円周, 輪 ②循環, 軌道 ③仲間, サークル 動 回る, 囲む
- **citizen** 名 ①市民, 国民 ②住民, 民間人
- **city** 名 ①都市, 都会 ②《the-》(全)市民
- **City Square** シティスクエア
- **civilization** 名 文明, 文明人(化) **ancient civilization** 古代文明
- **claim** 動 ①主張する ②要求する, 請求する 名 ①主張, 断言 ②要求, 請求
- **class** 名 ①学級, 組, 階級 ②授業 動 分類する, 等級をつける
- **Class e-Times** クラスeタイムス《オンライン学級新聞の誌名》
- **classical** 形 古典の, クラシックの
- **classmate** 名 同級生, 級友
- **classroom** 名 教室, クラス
- **claw** 名 鉤爪 動 爪で引っかく
- **clean** 形 ①きれいな, 清潔な ②正当な 動 掃除する 副 ①きれいに ②まったく, すっかり
- **cleaner** 形 clean (きれいな)の比較級 副 clean のの比較級 名 ①掃除する人, クリーニング店主 ②掃除機, クリーナー
- **cleanliness** 名 清潔, きれい好き
- **clear** 形 ①はっきりした, 明白な ②澄んだ ③(よく)晴れた 動 ①はっきりさせる ②片づける ③晴れる 副 ①はっきりと ②すっかり, 完全に
- **cleared land** 裸地
- **clearly** 副 ①明らかに, はっきりと ②《返答に用いて》そのとおり
- **click** 名 ①カチッという音 ②(マウスの)クリック 動 ①カチッと音がする[音をさせる] ②(ボタンを)カチッと押す, クリックする
- **client** 名 依頼人, 顧客, クライアント
- **climb** 動 登る, 徐々に上がる 名 登ること, 上昇
- **clip** 動 (はさみなどで)切り取る, 切り抜く 名 刈り込み, 切り抜き
- **clock** 名 掛け[置き]時計
- **close** 形 ①近い ②親しい ③狭い 副 ①接近して ②密集して **bring close** 〜に近づける 動 ①閉まる, 閉める ②終える, 閉店する
- **closely** 副 ①密接に ②念入りに, 詳しく ③ぴったりと
- **clothes** 動 clothe (服を着せる)の3人称単数現在 名 衣服, 身につけるもの
- **clothing** 動 clothe (服を着せる)の現在分詞 名 衣類, 衣料品
- **cloudy** 形 ①曇った, 雲の多い ②はっきりしない, 濁った
- **club** 名 ①クラブ, (同好)会 ②こん棒 動 こん棒で打つ[なぐる]
- **coach** 名 ①長距離用のバス ②(鉄道の)普通客車 ③大型四輪馬車 ④コーチ, 指導者
- **coat** 名 ①コート ②(動物の)毛 動 ①表面を覆う ②上着を着せる
- **cocoa** 名 ココア
- **code** 名 ①法典 ②規準, 慣例 ③コード, 番号 動 コード化する
- **coffee** 名 コーヒー
- **coincidence** 名 同時発生, 一致, 合致
- **cola** 名 コーラ《炭酸飲料》

WORD LIST

- **cold** 形①寒い,冷たい ②冷淡な,冷静な 名①寒さ,冷たさ ②風邪 cold front 寒冷前線
- **coldly** 副冷たく,よそよそしく
- **Cole** 名コール《人名》
- **collaborate** 動協力する,共同する
- **collaboration** 名協力,協調,共同制作 in collaboration with ～と共同して
- **colleague** 名同僚,仲間,同業者
- **collect** 動①集める,集金する ②まとめる 形着払いの
- **collector** 名集める人,収集家 tax collector 税務署員
- **college** 名(単科)大学,(専門)学部,各種学校
- **color** 名①色,色彩 ②絵の具 ③血色 動色をつける
- **column** 名①コラム ②(新聞などの)縦の段[行・列] ③(円)柱
- **combination** 名①結合(状態,行為),団結 ②連合,同盟
- **combine** 動①結合する[させる] ②連合する,協力する 名合同,連合
- **come** 動①来る,行く,現れる ②(出来事が)起こる,生じる ③～になる ④comeの過去分詞 come about 起こる come in 中にはいる come into ～に入ってくる come off 取れる,はずれる come out of ～から出てくる come to be traded 取引されるようになる come to see ～が理解できるようになる come up with 考え出す,見つけ出す,～に追いつく come up 近づいてくる,上がって来る
- **comfortable** 形快適な,心地いい
- **command** 動命令する,指揮する 名命令,指揮(権) command of a basic vocabulary 基礎語彙力
- **comment** 名論評,解説,コメント 動論評する,注解する,コメントする
- **commercial** 形商業の,営利的な
- **commit** 動①委託する ②引き受ける ③(罪などを)犯す
- **common** 形①共通の,共同の ②普通の,平凡な ③一般の,公共の 名①共有地 ②公園 in common (with ～)(～と)共通して
- **commonly** 副一般に,通例
- **communicate** 動①知らせる,連絡する ②理解し合う
- **communication** 名伝えること,伝達,連絡
- **community** 名①団体,共同社会,地域社会 ②《the-》社会(一般),世間 ③共有,共同責任
- **company** 名①会社 ②交際,同席 ③友だち,仲間,一団,人の集まり
- **compare** 動①比較する,対照する ②たとえる 《be》compared with ～と比較して,～に比べれば
- **comparison** 名比較,対照
- **compassionate** 形思いやりのある,慈悲深い,心の優しい
- **compete** 動①競争する ②(競技に)参加する ③匹敵する
- **competition** 名競争,競合,コンペ
- **competitive** 形競争の,競争心の強い,(品質などが)他に負けない
- **competitor** 名競争相手,競争者
- **complain** 動①不平[苦情]を言う,ぶつぶつ言う ②(病状などを)訴える
- **complete** 形完全な,まったくの,完成した 動完成させる
- **completely** 副完全に,すっかり
- **compose** 動①構成する,《be-d of ～》～から成り立つ ②作曲する,(詩などを)書く
- **computer** 名コンピュータ
- **concentration** 名①集中,集中

力, 集合 ②濃縮, 濃度
- **concept** 名 ①概念, 観念, テーマ ②(計画案などの)基本的な方向
- **concern** 動 ①関係する,《be -ed in [with] 〜》〜に関係している ②心配させる,《be -ed about [for] 〜》〜を心配する 名 ①関心事 ②関心, 心配 ③関係, 重要性
- **concert** 名 ①音楽[演奏]会, コンサート ②一致, 協力
- **conclude** 動 ①終える, 完結する ②結論をドす
- **condition** 名 ①(健康)状態, 境遇 ②《-s》状況, 様子 ③条件 動 適応させる, 条件づける
- **conduct** 名 ①行い, 振る舞い ②指導, 指揮 動 ①指導する ②実施する, 処理[処置]する
- **conductor** 名 指導者, 案内者, 管理者, 指揮者, (伝)導体 poor conductor of heat 熱を伝導しない
- **confidence** 名 自信, 確信, 信頼, 信用度
- **confident** 形 自信のある, 自信に満ちた
- **congratulations** 間 おめでとう!
- **connect** 動 つながる, つなぐ, 関係づける
- **conservation** 名 保護, 保管, 保存
- **consider** 動 ①考慮する, 〜しようと思う ②(〜と)みなす ③気にかける, 思いやる
- **considerably** 副 かなり, 相当に
- **considerate** 形 思いやりのある
- **consideration** 名 ①考慮, 考察 ②考慮すべきこと
- **consist** 動 ①《- of 〜》(部分・要素から)成る ②《- in 〜》〜に存在する, 〜にある
- **consistent** 形 首尾一貫した, 筋の通った, しっかりした
- **constantly** 副 絶えず, いつも, 絶え間なく
- **contact** 名 ①接触, 交渉 ②関係, 連絡 動 ①接触する ②連絡をとる
- **contain** 動 ①含む, 入っている ②(感情などを)抑える
- **content** 名 ①《-s》中身, 内容, 目次 ②満足 形 満足して 動 満足する[させる]
- **continue** 動 続く, 続ける, (中断後)再開する, (ある方向に)移動していく
- **contrast** 名 対照, 対比 in contrast 対照的に, その一方 動 対照させる, よい対象となる
- **contribute** 動 ①貢献する ②寄稿する ③寄付する contribute to 〜 に貢献する, 〜の一因となる
- **control** 動 ①管理[支配]する ②抑制する, コントロールする 名 ①管理, 支配(力) ②抑制 get out of control 手のつけられない状態になる keep control over 〜を管理下に置いておく
- **controller** 名 ①会計監査(役), 管理者 ②制御装置, コントローラー
- **convenience** 名 便利(さ), 便利なもの, 利便性 convenience store コンビニ
- **convenient** 形 便利な, 好都合な
- **conversation** 名 会話, 会談
- **convert** 動 変える, 転換する, 改宗させる
- **cooking** 動 cook (料理する)の過去, 過去分詞 名 料理(法), クッキング
- **cool** 形 ①涼しい, 冷えた ②冷静な ③かっこいい 動 ①涼しくなる, 冷える ②冷静になる 名 涼しさ, 涼しい場所
- **cooperation** 名 ①協力, 協業, 協調 ②協同組合
- **cooperative** 形 協力的な, 協同の, 協同組合の 名 生活協同組合

Word List

- **corner** 名 ①曲がり角, 角 ②すみ, はずれ 動 ①窮地に追いやる ②買い占める ③角を曲がる
- **corporation** 名 法人, (株式) 会社, 公団, 社団法人
- **Cosmos Line Ferry** コスモスライン・フェリー
- **cost** 名 ①値段, 費用 ②損失, 犠牲 動 (金・費用が) かかる, (~を) 要する, (人に金額を) 費やさせる
- **Costa Rica** コスタリカ共和国
- **could** 動 ①can (~できる) の過去 ②《控え目な推量・可能性・願望などを表す》Could you ~? ~してくださいますか。
- **count** 動 ①数える ②(~を…と) みなす ③重要 [大切] である count on ~を頼りにする 名 計算, 総計, 勘定
- **countless** 形 無数の, 数え切れない
- **country** 名 ①国 ②《the -》田舎, 郊外 ③地域, 領域, 分野 形 田舎の, 野暮な
- **countryside** 名 地方, 田舎
- **couple** 名 ①2つ, 対 ②夫婦, 一組 ③数個 動 つなぐ, つながる, 関連させる
- **courage** 名 勇気, 度胸
- **course** 名 ①進路, 方向 ②経過, 成り行き ③科目, 講座 ④策, 方策 of course もちろん, 当然
- **court** 名 ①中庭, コート ②法廷, 裁判所 ③宮廷, 宮殿 food court 飲食用カウンター
- **cousin** 名 いとこ, よく似た人 [物]
- **cover** 動 ①覆う, 包む, 隠す ②扱う, (~に) わたる, 及ぶ ③代わりを務める ④補う 名 覆い, カバー
- **cow** 名 雌牛, 乳牛
- **Cracow Music School** クラコウ音楽学校
- **crash** 動 ①(人・乗り物が) 衝突する, 墜落する ②大きな音を立ててぶつかる [壊れる] 名 ①激突, 墜落 ②(壊れるときの) すさまじい音
- **create** 動 創造する, 生み出す, 引き起こす
- **crew** 名 クルー, 乗組員, 搭乗員
- **crew cut** クルーカット, 角刈り
- **criticism** 名 批評, 非難, 反論, 評論
- **crop** 名 作物, 収穫 動 収穫する, 刈り込む
- **cross** 動 ①横切る, 渡る ②じゃまする ③十字を切る 名 十字架, 十字形のもの 形 交差した
- **crowd** 動 群がる, 混雑する 名 群集, 雑踏, 多数, 聴衆
- **crowded** 動 crowd (群がる) の過去, 過去分詞 形 混雑した, 満員の
- **crucial** 形 ①重大な, 決定的な ②致命的な, 正念場で
- **cry** 動 泣く, 叫ぶ, 大声を出す, 嘆く cry out 叫ぶ 名 泣き声, 叫び, かっさい
- **cuisine** 名 料理, 料理法 Japanese cuisine 日本料理
- **culture** 名 ①文化 ②教養 ③耕作, 栽培 youth culture 若者文化 動 耕す, 栽培する
- **Culture Day** 文化の日
- **curled hair** 巻き毛, カールした髪
- **currently** 副 今のところ, 現在
- **curriculum** 名 履修科目, カリキュラム
- **curved line** 曲線
- **customer** 名 顧客
- **customer-service** 形 顧客サービス, アフター・サービス
- **cut** 動 ①切る, 刈る ②短縮する, 削る ③cutの過去, 過去分詞 名 ①切ること, 切り傷 ②削除 ③ヘアスタイル
- **cutting** 動 cut (切る) の現在分詞 名 ①切ること, 裁断, カッティング

②(新聞などの)切り抜き, (挿し木用の)切り枝
- **cycling** 名 サイクリング

D

- **daily** 形 毎日の, 日常の 副 毎日, 日ごとに 名 (-lies) 日刊新聞
- **dairy** 名 搾乳所, 酪農場, 乳製品販売[製造]所
- **Dan Wright** ダン・ライト《人名》
- **dance** 動 踊る, ダンスをする 名 ダンス, ダンスパーティー
- **dancing** 動 dance (踊る)の現在分詞 名 ダンス, 舞踏
- **dangerous** 形 危険な, 有害な
- **dark** 形 ①暗い, 闇の ②(色が)濃い, (髪が)黒い ③陰うつな 名 ①《the -》暗がり, 闇 ②日暮れ, 夜 ③暗い色[影]
- **darling** 名 ①最愛の人 ②あなた《呼びかけ》
- **data** 名 データ, 情報
- **date** 名 ①日付, 年月日 ②デート out of date 時代遅れの, 古くさい 動 ①日付を記す ②デートする
- **daughter** 名 娘
- **day** 名 ①日中, 昼間 ②日, 期日 ③《-s》時代, 生涯 one day (過去の)ある日, (未来の)いつか
- **dead** 形 ①死んでいる, 活気のない, 枯れた ②まったくの 名《the -》死者たち, 故人 副 完全に, まったく
- **deaf** 形 耳が聞こえない 名 耳が聞こえない人
- **deal** 動 分配する deal with ～に対応する 名 ①取引, 扱い ②(不特定の)量, 額 a good [great] deal (of ～) かなり, ずいぶん・大量 (の～), 多額 (の～)
- **dealt** 動 deal (分配する)の過去, 過去分詞

- **dear** 形 いとしい, 親愛なる, 大事な 名 ねえ, あなた《呼びかけ》 間 まあ, おや
- **decide** 動 決定[決意]する, (～しようと)決める, 判決を下す
- **decision** 名 ①決心 ②決定, 判決 ③決断(力)
- **deck** 名 (船の)デッキ, 甲板, 階, 床 observation deck 展望台
- **decoration** 名 装飾, 飾りつけ
- **decrease** 動 減少する 名 減少
- **dedication** 名 装飾
- **deep** 形 ①深い, 深さ～の ②深遠な ③濃い 副 深く
- **deepen** 動 深くする, 深める
- **deeply** 副 深く, 非常に
- **definitely** 副 ①限定的に, 明確に, 確実に ②まったくそのとおり
- **definition** 名 定義, 限定
- **degree** 名 ①程度, 階級, 位, 身分 ②(温度・角度の)度
- **demand** 動 ①要求する, 尋ねる ②必要とする 名 ①要求, 請求 ②需要
- **demanding** 形 要求が厳しい
- **demonstrate** 動 ①デモをする ②実演する ③実証する
- **depend** 動 depend on ①～を頼る, ～をあてにする ②～による
- **depression** 名 ①不景気, 不況 ②憂うつ, 意気消沈
- **depth** 名 深さ, 奥行き, 深いところ
- **describe** 動 (言葉で)描写する, 特色を述べる, 説明する
- **design** 動 設計する, 企てる 名 デザイン, 設計(図)
- **designer** 名 デザイナー, 設計者
- **desk** 名 ①机, 台 ②受付(係), フロント, カウンター, 部局
- **despite** 前 ～にもかかわらず
- **destination** 名 行き先, 目的地

WORD LIST

- **destroy** 動 破壊する, 絶滅させる, 無効にする
- **destruction** 名 破壊(行為・状態) human destruction 人為的破壊
- **detailed** 動 detail(詳しく述べる)の過去, 過去分詞 形 詳細な, 詳しい
- **determine** 動 ①決心する[させる] ②決定する[させる] ③測定する
- **develop** 動 ①発達する[させる] ②開発する
- **development** 名 ①発達, 発展 ②開発
- **devote** 動 ①(~を…に)捧げる ②《- oneself to ~》~に専念する
- **dictionary** 名 辞書, 辞典
- **did** 動 do(~をする)の過去 助 do の過去
- **die** 動 死ぬ, 消滅する
- **diet** 名 ①食べ物, 食事 ②食習慣 ③ダイエット, 食餌療法 ④国会, 議会, 正式な会議 形 低カロリーの 動 ①ダイエットする, 食事制限をする ②食べ物を与える ③ダイエットさせる
- **dietary** 形 食べ物の, 規定食の 名 規定食, 特別食
- **dieting** 名 ダイエット, 食事療法をすること
- **differ** 動 異なる, 違う, 意見が合わない
- **difference** 名 違い, 相違, 差
- **different** 形 異なった, 違った, 別の, さまざまな
- **differently** 副 (~と)異なって, 違って
- **difficult** 形 困難な, むずかしい, 扱いにくい
- **digitally** 形 デジタル処理で
- **dinner** 名 ①ディナー, 夕食 ②夕食[食事]会, 祝宴
- **direction** 名 ①方向, 方角 ②《-s》指示, 説明書 ③指導, 指揮
- **directly** 副 ①じかに ②まっすぐに ③ちょうど
- **disadvantaged** 形 恵まれない, 不利な条件に置かれた
- **disagree** 動 異議を唱える, 反対する
- **disappear** 動 見えなくなる, 姿を消す, なくなる
- **discipline** 名 規律, しつけ 動 訓練する, しつける
- **disco** 名 ディスコ《音楽・ダンス》
- **discover** 動 発見する, 気づく
- **discovery** 名 発見
- **discussion** 名 討議, 討論
- **disease** 名 病気, 不健全な状態
- **dish** 名 ①大皿 ②料理
- **disorder** 名 混乱, 無秩序, 乱雑 動 乱す
- **distance** 名 距離, 隔たり, 遠方
- **distant** 形 ①遠い, 隔たった ②よそよそしい, 距離のある
- **distracting** 形 目[注意]をそらさせる
- **distress** 名 悩み, 苦痛 動 悩ませる
- **distribute** 動 ①分配[配布]する ②流通させる
- **dive** 動 ①飛び込む, もぐる ②急降下する[させる] 名 飛び込み, ダイビング
- **diversify** 動 多様化する, 多角化する
- **divide** 動 分かれる, 分ける, 割れる, 割る
- **dizzy** 形 めまいがする, 目が回る, くらくらする
- **do** 助 ①《ほかの動詞とともに用いて現在形の否定文・疑問文をつくる》 ②《同じ動詞を繰り返す代わりに用いる》 ③《動詞を強調するのに用いる》 動 ~をする do away with ~を廃止する do with ~を処理する do without ~なしですませる

175

- **doctor** 名医者, 博士(号) **medical doctor** 医師
- **document** 名書類, 文書, 資料 動文書化する, 記録する
- **does** 動do(〜をする)の3人称単数現在 助doの3人称単数現在
- **dog** 名犬
- **dollar** 名ドル《米国などの通貨単位, 記号$》
- **dolphin** 名イルカ
- **done** 動do(〜をする)の過去分詞
- **door** 名①ドア, 戸 ②一軒, 一戸
- **dot** 名①点, 小数点 ②水玉(模様)
- **double** 形①2倍の, 二重の ②対の 副①2倍に ②対で 動①2倍になる[する] ②兼ねる
- **doubtful** 形疑わしい, あやふやな, おぼつかない, (人物が)いかがわしい
- **down** 副①下へ, 降りて, 低くなって ②倒れて 前〜の下方へ, 〜を下って 形下方の, 下りの
- **download** 動ダウンロードする
- **Dr.** 名〜博士, 《医者に対して》〜先生
- **dramatic** 形劇的な, 印象的な, 劇の
- **draw** 動①引く, 引っ張る ②描く ③引き分けになる[する] 名呼び物, 客を引きつけるもの
- **drawn** 動draw(引く)の過去分詞
- **dress** 名ドレス, 衣服, 正装 **dress code** 服装規定 動①服を着る[着せる] ②飾る
- **drink** 動飲む, 飲酒する 名飲み物, 酒, 1杯
- **drive** 動①車で行く, (車を)運転する ②追いやる, (ある状態に)する 名ドライブ
- **driver** 名①運転手 ②(馬車の)御者
- **driving** 動drive(車で行く)の現在分詞 形①推進する, 精力的な ②運転用の **driving force** 原動力, 立役者 名運転
- **drop** 動①(ぽたぽた)落ちる, 落とす ②下がる, 下げる **drop in** ちょっと立ち寄る 名しずく, 落下
- **drove** 動drive(車で行く)の過去
- **drug** 名薬, 麻薬, 麻酔薬
- **duck** 名カモ, アヒル 動頭を下げる, 身をかわす
- **due** 形予定された, 期日のきている, 支払われるべき **due to** 〜によって, 〜が原因で 名当然の権利
- **dull** 形退屈な, 鈍い, くすんだ, ぼんやりした 動鈍くなる[する]
- **during** 前〜の間(ずっと)
- **dust** 名ちり, ほこり, ごみ, 粉 動ちり[ほこり]を払う
- **dusty** 形ほこりだらけの

E

- **each** 形それぞれの, 各自の 代それぞれ, 各自 **each other** お互いに **next to each other** 隣同士に 副それぞれに
- **ear** 名耳, 聴覚 **inner ear** 内なる耳
- **early** 形①(時間や時期が)早い ②初期の, 幼少の, 若い 副①早く, 早めに ②初期に, 初めのころに
- **earn** 動①儲ける, 稼ぐ ②(名声を)博す
- **earning** 名収入, 所得
- **earth** 名①《the -》地球 ②大地, 陸地, 土 ③この世 **on earth** 世界中で, 地上で, 《疑問・否定文で》いったい全体, およそ
- **ease** 名安心, 気楽 動安心させる, 楽にする, ゆるめる
- **easily** 副①容易に, たやすく, 苦もなく ②気楽に
- **east** 名《the -》東, 東部, 東方 形東の, 東方[東部]の

Word List

- **easy** 形①やさしい,簡単な ②気楽な,くつろいだ take it easy 気楽にやる
- **eating habit** 食習慣,食生活
- **economic** 形経済学の,経済上の economic value 経済的価値
- **education** 名教育,教養
- **educational** 形教育(上)の
- **effect** 名①影響,効果,結果 ②実施,発効 in effect 有効な,事実上 動もたらす,達成する
- **effective** 形効果的である,有効である
- **efficiency** 名①能率,効率 ②能力
- **efficient** 形①効率的な,有効な ②有能な,敏腕な
- **effort** 名努力(の成果)
- **Eiffel Tower** エッフェル塔《仏,1964》
- **eight** 名8(の数字),8人[個] 形8の,8人[個]の
- **eighteenth** 名第18番目(の人[もの]),18日 形第18番目の
- **eighteenth-century** 18世紀
- **eighty** 名80(の数字),80人[個] 形80の,80人[個]の
- **either** 形①(2つのうち)どちらかの ②どちらでも 代どちらも,どちらでも 副①どちらか《否定文で》~もまた(…ない) 接《- ~ or …》~かまたは…か
- **elder** 形年上の,年長の
- **elderly** 形かなり年配の,初老の 名《the -》お年寄り
- **elementary** 形①初歩の ②単純な,簡単な
- **Elena** 名エレナ《人名》
- **elevator** 名エレベーター
- **eleventh** 名第11番目(の人[物]),11日 形第11番目の
- **Ella** 名エラ《人名》

- **else** 副①そのほかに[の],代わりに ②さもないと or else さもないと
- **emerge** 動現れる,浮かび上がる,明らかになる
- **emphasis** 名強調,強勢,重要性
- **emphasize** 動①強調する ②重視する
- **employ** 動①(人を)雇う,使う ②利用する 名雇用,職業
- **empty** 形①空の,空いている ②(心などが)ぼんやりした,無意味な 動空になる[する],注ぐ
- **enable** 動(~することを)可能にする,容易にする
- **encounter** 動(思いがけなく)出会う,遭う 名遭遇,(思いがけない)出会い
- **encourage** 動①勇気づける ②促進する,助長する
- **encyclopedia** 名百科事典
- **end** 名①終わり,終末,死 ②果て,末,端 ③「in the end とうとう,最後には 動終わる,終える
- **endanger** 動危険にさらす,脅かす
- **Endeavour** 名エンデバー号《スペースシャトルの名》
- **ending** 動end(終わる)の現在分詞 名終わり,結末
- **endlessly** 副果てしなく,無限に
- **energy** 名①力,勢い ②元気,精力,エネルギー
- **engine** 名エンジン,機関,(精巧な)機械装置
- **engineering** 名工学
- **England** 名①イングランド ②英国
- **English** 名①英語 ②《the -》英国人 形①英語の ②英国(人)の
- **English-Japanese** 名英和
- **enjoy** 動楽しむ,享受する enjoy oneself 楽しく過ごす,楽しむ

177

- **enjoyment** 名 楽しむこと, 喜び
- **enormous** 形 ばく大な, 非常に大きい, 巨大な
- **enough** 形 十分な, (～するに)足る 名 十分な(量・数), たくさん **enough of ～** はもうたくさん 副(～できる)だけ, 十分に, まったく **cannot ～ enough** いくら～してもしたりない
- **enroll** 動 登録する, 入会する, 入学する
- **enter** 動 ①入る, 入会[入学]する[させる] ②記入する ③(考えなどが)(心・頭に)浮かぶ
- **entertainment** 名 ①楽しみ, 娯楽 ②もてなし, 歓待
- **enthusiasm** 名 情熱, 熱意, 熱心
- **enthusiastic** 形 熱狂的な, 熱烈な
- **entire** 形 全体の, 完全な, まったくの
- **entrance** 名 ①入り口, 入場 ②開始
- **entry** 名 入ること, 入り口
- **environment** 名 ①環境 ②周囲(の状況), 情勢 **living environment** 生活環境 **outdoor environment** 屋外環境
- **equal** 形 等しい, 均等な, 平等な 動 匹敵する, 等しい 名 同等のもの[人]
- **equally** 副 等しく, 平等に
- **equipment** 名 装置, 機材, 道具, 設備
- **equivalence** 名 等値, 同等, 等価
- **equivalent** 形 ①同等の, 等しい ②同意義の 名 同等のもの, 等価なもの
- **Eri** 名 絵里《人名》
- **escalator** 名 エスカレーター
- **escape** 動 逃げる, 免れる, もれる 名 逃亡, 脱出, もれ
- **especially** 副 特別に, とりわけ

- **essay** 名 エッセイ, 随筆
- **essential** 形 本質的な, 必須の 《**be**》**essential to** ～にとって絶対必要である 名 本質, 要点, 必需品
- **establish** 動 確立する, 立証する, 設置[設立]する
- **estimate** 動 ①見積もる ②評価する 名 ①見積もり(書) ②評価
- **Europe** 名 ヨーロッパ
- **European** 名 ヨーロッパ人 形 ヨーロッパ(人)の
- **Eva** 名 エヴァ《人名》
- **even** 副 ①《強意》～でさえも, ～ですら, いっそう, なおさら ②平等に **even if** たとえ～でも **even though** ～であるのに, たとえ～でも 形 ①平らな, 水平の ②等しい, 均一の ③落ち着いた 動 平らになる[する], 釣り合いがとれる
- **evening** 名 ①夕方, 晩 ②《the [one's] －》末期, 晩年, 衰退期
- **evenly** 副 等しく, 均等に, 対等に
- **event** 名 出来事, 事件, イベント **at all events** ともかく, いずれにしても **in any event** 何が起ころうとも
- **eventually** 副 結局は
- **ever** 副 ①今までに, これまで, かつて, いつまでも ②《強意》いったい
- **every** 形 ①どの～も, すべての, あらゆる ②毎～, ～ごとの
- **everybody** 代 誰でも, 皆
- **everyday** 形 毎日の, 日々の
- **everyone** 代 誰でも, 皆
- **everything** 代 すべてのこと[もの], 何でも, 何もかも
- **evidence** 名 ①証拠, 証人 ②形跡
- **exactly** 副 ①正確に, 厳密に, ちょうど ②まったくそのとおり
- **exaggerate** 動 大げさに言う[考える], 誇張する
- **examine** 動 試験する, 調査[検査]

WORD LIST

する, 診察する

- **example** 名 例, 見本, 模範 for example たとえば
- **excellent** 形 優れた, 優秀な
- **except** 前 ～を除いて, ～のほかは except for ～を除いて, ～がなければ 接 ～ということを除いて
- **exception** 名 例外, 除外, 異論
- **exchange** 動 交換する, 両替する 名 ①交換, 両替 ②小切手, 為替 exchange student 交換留学生
- **exciting** 動 excite (興奮する)の現在分詞 形 興奮させる, わくわくさせる
- **exercise** 名 ①運動, 体操 ②練習 physical exercise 体操 動 ①運動する, 練習する ②影響を及ぼす
- **exhibit** 動 展示する, 見せる, 示す 名 表示, 展示, 展覧会, 展示品
- **exit** 名 出口, 退去 動 退出する, 退去する
- **expand** 動 広げる, 拡張[拡大]する
- **expect** 動 予期[予測]する, (当然のこととして)期待する
- **expensive** 形 高価な, ぜいたくな
- **experience** 名 経験, 体験 動 経験[体験]する
- **expert** 名 専門家, 熟練者, エキスパート 形 熟練した, 専門の
- **explain** 動 説明する, 明らかにする, 釈明[弁明]する
- **explanation** 名 ①説明, 解説, 釈明 ②解釈, 意味
- **explore** 動 探検[調査]する, 切り開く
- **exposed** 動 expose (さらす)の過去, 過去分詞 《be》 exposed to ～にさらされる, ～に触れる 形 ①雨風[光, 攻撃, 危険]にさらされた ②露出した, 無防備な ③露呈した, 発覚した
- **exposure** 名 ①さらされる ②暴露, 暴くこと
- **express** 動 表現する, 述べる 形 ①明白な ②急行の 名 速達便, 急行列車 副 速達で, 急行で
- **expression** 名 ①表現, 表示, 表情 ②言い回し, 語句 beyond expression 言い表せないほど
- **extensive** 形 広い, 広範囲に渡る, 大規模な
- **extent** 名 範囲, 程度, 広さ, 広がり
- **extinct** 形 消えた, 絶滅した
- **extra** 形 余分の, 臨時の 名 ①余分なもの ②エキストラ 副 余分に
- **extreme** 形 極端な, 極度の, いちばん端の 名 極端
- **extremely** 副 非常に, 極度に
- **eye** 名 ①目, 視力 ②眼識, 観察力 ③注目 keep an eye on ～から目を離さない take one's eyes off ～から目をそらす

F

- **face** 名 ①顔, 顔つき ②外観, 外見 ③(時計の)文字盤, (建物の)正面 face away from ～から見て外に向く face to face 面と向かって, 差し向かいで in (the) face of ～の面前で, ～に直面して 動 直面する, 立ち向かう
- **facility** 名 ①《-ties》施設, 設備 ②器用さ, 容易さ
- **fact** 名 事実, 真相 in fact 実は, 要するに
- **factor** 名 要因, 要素, 因子
- **failing** 名 失敗, 不手際
- **fair** 形 ①正しい, 公平[正当]な ②快晴の ③色白の, 金髪の ④かなりの ⑤《古》美しい 副 ①公平に, きれいに ②見事に
- **Fairtrade** 名 公平取引, フェアトレード

- **fall** 動①落ちる, 倒れる ②(値段・温度が)下がる ③(ある状態に)急に陥る 名①落下, 墜落 ②滝 ③崩壊 ④秋
- **fallen** 動 fall (落ちる) の過去分詞 形落ちた, 倒れた
- **fame** 名評判, 名声
- **familiar** 形①親しい, 親密な ②《be》familiar with ~に精通している ③普通の, いつもの, おなじみの
- **family** 名家族, 家庭, 一門, 家柄
- **famous** 形有名な, 名高い
- **far** 副①遠くに, はるかに, 離れて ②《比較級を強めて》ずっと, はるかに as far as ~と同じくらい遠く, ~まで, ~する限り(では) by far はるかに, 断然 far from ~から遠く, ~どころか so far 今までのところ, これまでは so far as ~する限り 形遠い, 向こうの 名遠方
- **farewell** 名別れ, 別れのあいさつ, 送別会 間さようなら, ごきげんよう
- **farm** 名農場, 農家 farm truck 農業用トラック 動(~を)耕作する
- **farmer** 名農民, 農場経営者
- **fascinate** 動魅惑する, うっとりさせる
- **fashion** 名①流行, 方法, はやり ②流行のもの(特に服装)
- **fashionable** 形①流行の ②上流社会の
- **fast** 形①(速度が)速い ②(時計が)進んでいる ③しっかりした 副①速く, 急いで ②(時計が)進んで ③しっかりと, ぐっすりと
- **fat** 形①太った ②脂っこい ③分厚い 名脂肪, 肥満
- **favor** 名①好意, えこひいき ②格別のはからい in favor of ~に賛成して 動好意を示す, 賛成する
- **favored** 形好まれている
- **favorite** 名お気に入り(の人[物]) 形お気に入りの, ひいきの

- **fear** 名①恐れ ②心配, 不安 動①恐れる ②心配する
- **fearlessness** 名恐怖心のなさ
- **feather** 名羽,《-s》羽毛
- **feature** 名①特徴, 特色 ②顔の一部,《-s》顔立ち ③(ラジオ・テレビ・新聞などの)特集 動①(~の)特徴になる ②呼び物にする
- **feel** 動感じる, (~と)思う feel for ~に同情する, ~を手さぐりで探す feel like ~がほしい, ~したい気がする, ~のような感じがする
- **feelingly** 副感情を込めて
- **feet** 名①foot (足) の複数 ②フィート《長さの単位。約30cm》
- **fellow** 名①仲間, 同僚 ②人, やつ 形仲間の, 同士の
- **felt** 動 feel (感じる) の過去, 過去分詞 名フェルト 形フェルト(製)の
- **female** 形女性の, 婦人の, 雌の 名婦人, 雌
- **ferry** 名渡し場, フェリーボート 動船で渡す, フェリーで川を渡る
- **few** 形①ほとんどない, 少数の(~しかない) ②《a-》少数の, 少しはある not [quite] a few かなり多くの 代少数の人[物]
- **field** 名①野原, 田畑, 広がり ②(研究)分野 ③競技場
- **fifteen** 名15(の数字), 15人[個] 形15の, 15人[個]の
- **fifth** 名第5番目(の人[物]), 5日 形第5番目の
- **fifties** 名50歳台
- **fifty** 名50(の数字), 50人[個] 形50の, 50人[個]の
- **fight** 動(~と)戦う, 争う 名①戦い, 争い, けんか ②闘志, ファイト
- **figure** 名①人[物]の姿, 形 ②図(形) ③数字 動①描写する, 想像する ②計算する ③目立つ, (~として)現れる figure out (問題などを)解く, 理解する

180

WORD LIST

- **file** 名 ファイル, 書類綴じ, 縦列 動 ①とじ込む, 保管する ②削り取る, やすりをかける
- **fill** 動 ①満ちる, 満たす ②《be -ed with ~》~でいっぱいである
- **final** 形 最後の, 決定的な 名 ①最後のもの ②期末[最終]試験 ③《-s》決勝戦
- **finally** 副 最後に, ついに, 結局
- **find** 動 ①見つける ②(~と)わかる, 気づく, ~と考える ③得る
- **find-the-right-word** 形 正しい言葉を見つける
- **finding** 動 find (見つける)の現在分詞 名 ①発見 ②《-s》発見物, 調査結果 ③《-s》認定, 決定, 答申
- **fine** 形 ①元気な ②美しい, りっぱな, 申し分ない, 結構な ③晴れた ④細かい, 微妙な 副 りっぱに, 申し分なく 動 罰金を科す 名 罰金
- **finger** 名 (手の)指 index finger 人差し指 middle finger 中指 動 指でさわる
- **fingernail** 名 指のつめ
- **finish** 動 終わる, 終える 名 終わり, 最後
- **finished** 動 finish (終わる)の過去, 過去分詞 形 ①終わった, 仕上がった ②洗練された ③もうだめになった
- **fire** 名 ①火, 炎, 火事 ②砲火, 攻撃 動 ①発射する, 解雇する ②火をつける
- **firm** 形 堅い, しっかりした, 断固とした 副 しっかりと
- **first** 名 最初, 第一(の人・物) at first 最初は, 初めのうちは 形 ①第一の, 最初の ②最も重要な 副 第一に, 最初に first of all 何よりもまず
- **fish** 名 魚 動 釣りをする
- **fist** 名 こぶし, げんこつ
- **fit** 形 ①適正な, 相応な ②体の調子がよい 動 合致[適合]する, 合致させる 名 発作, けいれん, 一時的興奮

- **five** 名 5(の数字), 5人[個] 形 5の, 5人[個]の
- **fix** 動 ①固定する[させる] ②修理する ③決定する ④用意する, 整える
- **flat** 形 ①平らな ②しぼんだ, 空気の抜けた 副 ①平らに, 平たく ②きっかり flat against ~にぴったり接した 名 ①平面, 平地 ②アパート
- **float** 動 ①浮く, 浮かぶ ②漂流する ③(心に)浮かぶ ④《be ~ing》(うわさなどが)広まる 名 浮くもの, いかだ
- **floor** 名 床, 階
- **Florence** 名 フィレンツェ《イタリアの都市》
- **flow** 動 流れ出る, 流れる, あふれる flow off into 流れてる, 流れ去る 名 ①流出 ②流ちょう(なこと)
- **flowered** 形 花で覆われた, 花柄の
- **fluent** 形 流ちょうな, 流れる(ような)
- **fluently** 副 流ちょうに, ペラペラと
- **fly** 動 ①飛ぶ, 飛ばす ②(飛ぶように)過ぎる, 急ぐ 名 ①飛行 ②ハエ
- **flying fish** トビウオ
- **focus** 名 ①焦点, ピント ②関心の的, 着眼点 ③中心 動 ①焦点を合わせる ②(関心・注意を)集中させる 《be》focused on ~に集中している
- **follow** 動 ①ついていく, あとをたどる ②(~の)結果として起こる ③(忠告などに)従う ④理解できる
- **follower** 名 信奉者, 追随者
- **following** 動 follow (ついていく)の現在分詞 形 《the -》次の, 次に続く 名 《the -》下記のもの, 以下に述べるもの
- **food** 名 食物, えさ food court 飲食用カウンター
- **foot** 名 ①足, 足取り ②(山などの)ふもと, (物の)最下部, すそ ③フィート《長さの単位, 約30cm》

READINGS FROM THE NATIONAL CENTER TEST FOR ENGLISH

- **footprint** 名 足型, 足跡
- **for** 前 ①《目的・原因・対象》～にとって, ～のために[の], ～に対して ②《期間》～間 ③《代理》～の代わりに ④《方向》～へ(向かって) 接 というわけは～, なぜなら～だから
- **force** 名 力, 勢い driving force 原動力, 立役者 動 ①強制する, 力ずくで～する, 余儀なく～させる ②押しやる, 押し込む force out of ～から強制的に追い出す
- **forceful** 形 力強い, 説得力のある
- **forehead** 名 ひたい
- **foreign** 形 外国の, よその
- **foreigner** 名 外国人, 外国製品
- **forest** 名 森林
- **forget** 動 忘れる, 置き忘れる
- **form** 名 ①形, 形式 ②書式 take form (物事が)形をとる, 具体化する 動 形づくる
- **former** 形 ①前の, 先の, 以前の ②《the ー》(二者のうち)前者の
- **forth** 副 前へ, 外へ and so forth [on] など, その他 bring forth 生み出す
- **fortunately** 副 幸運にも
- **forty** 名 40(の数字), 40人[個] 形 40の, 40人[個]の
- **forward** 形 ①前方の, 前方へ向かう ②将来の ③先の 副 ①前方に ②将来に向けて ③先へ, 進んで look forward to ～[～ing]～を期待する 動 ①転送する ②進める 名 前衛
- **found** 動 ①find (見つける)の過去, 過去分詞
- **four** 名 4(の数字), 4人[個] 形 4の, 4人[個]の
- **four-lane** 4車線の(道路)
- **fourth** 名 第4番目(の人・物), 4日 形 第4番目の
- **France** 名 フランス《国名》
- **free** 形 ①自由な, 開放された, 自由に～できる ②暇で, (物が)空いている, 使える ③無料の 副 ①自由に ②無料で 動 自由にする, 解放する
- **freelance** 名 フリーランサー 形 フリーランスの, 自由契約の
- **freely** 副 自由に, 障害なしに
- **frequency** 名 ①頻繁に起こること, 頻発 ②頻度 ③周波数
- **frequently** 副 頻繁に, しばしば
- **fresh** 形 ①新鮮な, 生気のある ②さわやかな, 清純な ③新規の
- **friend** 名 友だち, 仲間
- **friendliness** 名 友情, 好意
- **friendly** 形 親しみのある, 親切な, 友情のこもった 副 友好的に, 親切に
- **friendship** 名 友人であること, 友情
- **frightening** 動 frighten (驚かせる)の現在分詞 形 恐ろしい, どきっとさせる
- **frog** 名 カエル(蛙)
- **from** 前 ①《出身・出発点・時間・順序・原料》～から ②《原因・理由》～がもとで from then on それ以来
- **front** 名 正面, 前 cold front 寒冷前線 in front of ～の前に, ～の正面に 形 正面の
- **fruit** 名 ①果実, 実 ②《-s》成果, 利益 動 実を結ぶ
- **frying pan** フライパン
- **full** 形 ①満ちた, いっぱいの, 満期の ②完全な, 盛りの, 充実した 名 全部
- **fully** 副 十分に, 完全に, まるまる
- **fun** 名 楽しみ, 冗談, おもしろいこと make fun of ～をからかう 動 からかう, ふざける
- **function** 動 働く, 機能する 名 機能, 作用
- **fundamental** 名 基本, 原理 形 基本の, 根本的な, 重要な
- **fur** 名 毛, 毛皮(製品)
- **further** 形 いっそう遠い, その上の,

なおいっそうの 副いっそう遠く, その上に, もっと 動促進する
- **furthermore** 副さらに, その上
- **future** 名未来, 将来 形未来の, 将来の
- **Future Swimmers Scholarship** 未来の水泳選手奨学金

G

- **gain** 動①得る, 増す ②進歩する, 進む 名①増加, 進歩 ②利益, 得ること, 獲得
- **gallery** 名美術館, 画廊, 回廊, 観客
- **game** 名ゲーム, 試合, 遊び, 競技 video game テレビゲーム 動賭けごとをする
- **gap** 名ギャップ, 隔たり, すき間 動すき間ができる
- **garden** 名庭, 庭園 動園芸をする, 庭いじりをする
- **Garstang** 名ガースタング《イギリスの町》
- **gas** 名①ガス, 気体 ②ガソリン 動ガス[ガソリン]を供給する
- **gas station** ガソリンスタンド
- **gather** 動①集まる, 集める ②生じる, 増す ③推測する
- **gave** 動 give (与える)の過去
- **gaze** 名凝視, 注視 動凝視する
- **geese** 名 goose (ガチョウ)の複数
- **gender** 名(社会的に決められた)性, 性別
- **general** 形①全体の, 一般の, 普通の ②おおよその ③(職位の)高い, 上級の in general 一般に, たいてい 名大将, 将軍
- **generally** 副①一般に, だいたい ②たいてい
- **generation** 名①同世代の人々 ②一世代 ②発生, 生成 for generations 何世代にも渡って
- **generous** 形①寛大な, 気前のよい ②豊富な
- **genetics** 名遺伝学
- **geographical** 形地理的な, 地理学上の
- **German** 形ドイツ(人・語)の 名①ドイツ人 ②ドイツ語
- **Germany** 名ドイツ《国名》
- **gerontology** 名老人学
- **Gerry** 名ジェリー《人名》
- **get** 動①得る, 手に入れる ②(ある状態)になる, いたる ③わかる, 理解する ④~させる, ~を(…の状態)にする ⑤(ある場所)に達する, 着く get along with (人)と仲良くする get around 広まる get bitten (虫に)さされる get going 取りかかる get on well with (人)とうまくやっていく get out of control 手のつけられない状態になる get ready 用意[支度]をする get thirsty のどが乾く get through 乗り切る get to know 知るようになる, 知り合う get to work 仕事を始める get used to ~に慣れる I get it. 分かりました。なるほど。 I'll get to that later. 後でその話をしましょう。
- **Gion** 名祇園《京都の繁華街》
- **girl** 名女の子, 少女
- **give** 動①与える, 贈る ②伝える, 述べる ③(~を)する can ever give (人)に与えられうる give in 降参する, (書類などを)提出する Give me a break. いいかげんにしろよ。 give off 発散する, 放つ give out 分配する, 発表する, 尽きる give up あきらめる, やめる
- **given** 動 give (与える)の過去分詞 形与えられた
- **glad** 形①うれしい, 喜ばしい ②《be – to ~》~してうれしい, 喜んで~する
- **glass** 名①ガラス(状のもの), コップ, グラス ②鏡, 望遠鏡 ③《-es》め

がね
- **gleaming** 形 キラリと光る
- **glorious** 形 ①栄誉に満ちた, 輝かしい ②荘厳な, すばらしい
- **glow** 動 ①(火が)白熱して輝く ②(体が)ほてる 名 ①白熱, 輝き ②ほてり, 熱情
- **go** 動 ①行く, 出かける ②動く ③進む, 経過する, いたる ④(ある状態に)なる be going to 〜するつもりである get going 取りかかる go by 経過する, 通り過ぎる go for 〜に出かける, 〜を取りに行く, 〜を好む go off 立ち去る, 発射する go on 続く, 続ける, 進んでいく go out 外へ出る go with 〜と一緒に行く, 〜と調和する, 〜にとても似合う go without 〜なしですませる
- **goal** 名 ①目的(地), 目標 ②決勝点, ゴール
- **gone** 動 go (行く)の過去分詞 形 去った, 使い果たした, 死んだ
- **good** 形 ①よい, 上手な, 優れた, 美しい ②(数量・程度が)かなりの, 相当な as good as 〜も同然で, ほとんど〜 be good at 〜[〜ing] 〜が得意である 間 よかった, わかった, よろしい 名 善, 徳, 益, 幸福
- **goods** 名 ①商品, 品物 ②貨物 ③財産, 家財道具, 所有物 ④服地, 布地
- **gorilla** 名 ゴリラ
- **gosh** 間 おやっ！, えっ！
- **gossip** 名 うわさ話, ゴシップ 動 うわさ話をする, 雑談する
- **got** 動 get (得る)の過去, 過去分詞
- **gotten** 動 get (得る)の過去分詞
- **government** 名 政治, 政府, 支配
- **grade** 名 学年, 等級, グレード, 成績 動 格付けする
- **grader** 名 ①等級をつける人 ②〜年生, 〜学年の生徒
- **gradually** 副 だんだんと
- **graduate** 動 卒業する 名 卒業生, (〜学校の)出身者
- **grammatical** 形 文法上の, 文法にのっとった
- **grand** 形 雄大な, 壮麗な
- **grandchildren** 名 grandchild (孫)の複数
- **granddaughter** 名 孫娘, 女の孫
- **grandfather** 名 祖父
- **grandmother** 名 祖母
- **grandpa** 名 祖父, おじいちゃん
- **grandparent** 名 祖父母
- **granted** 副 確かに
- **grape** 名 ブドウ
- **graph** 名 グラフ, 図表
- **grateful** 形 感謝する, ありがたく思う
- **gratitude** 名 感謝(の気持ち), 報恩の念
- **gray** 形 ①灰色の ②どんよりした, 憂うつな ③白髪の 名 灰色 動 灰色になる[する]
- **great** 形 ①大きい, 広大な, (量や程度が)たいへんな ②偉大な, 優れた ③すばらしい, おもしろい
- **green** 形 ①緑色の, 青々とした ②未熟な, 若い ③生き生きした 名 ①緑色 ②草地, 芝生, 野菜
- **Grodzinska** 名 グロドジンスカ《人名》
- **ground** 名 地面, 土, 土地 動 ①基づかせる ②着陸する ③grind (ひく)の過去, 過去分詞 形 (粉に)ひいた, すった
- **group** 名 集団, 群 動 集まる
- **grow** 動 ①成長する, 育つ, 育てる ②増大する, 大きくなる, (次第に〜)になる
- **growth** 名 成長, 発展 形 成長している
- **Guana** 名 グアナ《都市名》
- **guess** 動 ①推測する, 言い当てる ②(〜と)思う Guess what. あのね, 何だと思う？ 知ってるかい？ 名 推

定, 憶測
- **guide** 動(道)案内する, 導く 名 ①ガイド, 手引き, 入門書 ②案内人
- **guidebook** 名旅行[観光]案内書, ガイドブック, 手引き
- **guitar** 名ギター

H

- **habit** 名習慣, 癖, 気質 be in the habit of ~ing ~する習慣がある
- **had** 動have(持つ)の過去, 過去分詞 助haveの過去《過去完了の文をつくる》 had better ~するほうがよい, ~しなさい
- **hair** 名髪, 毛
- **hairstyle** 名ヘアスタイル, 髪型
- **hairy** 形毛むくじゃらの, 毛製の
- **Hakata** 名博多《都市名》
- **half** 名半分 形半分の, 不完全な 副半分, なかば, 不十分に
- **half-circle** 形半円(の)
- **hall** 名公会堂, ホール, 大広間, 玄関
- **hallway** 名玄関, 廊下
- **hand** 名 ①手 ②(時計の)針 ③援助の手, 助け at hand 近くに, すぐ使えるように on the other hand 他方では, 一方 動手渡す hand in 差し出す, 提出する hand out 配る hand over 引き渡す, 譲渡する
- **handicapped** 動handicap(ハンデをつける)の過去, 過去分詞 形身体に障害のある, ハンディキャップのある
- **handle** 名取っ手, 握り 動①手を触れる ②操縦する, 取り扱う
- **happen** 動①(出来事が)起こる, 生じる ②偶然[たまたま]~する
- **happiness** 名幸せ, 喜び
- **happy** 形幸せな, うれしい, 幸運な, 満足して
- **hard** 形①堅い ②激しい, むずかしい ③熱心な, 勤勉な ④無情な, 耐えがたい, 厳しい, きつい 副①一生懸命に ②激しく ③堅く
- **hare** 名野ウサギ
- **harmful** 形害を及ぼす, 有害な
- **harmonious** 形調和のとれた, 仲むつまじい
- **harmony** 名調和, 一致, ハーモニー
- **harvest** 名①収穫(物), 刈り入れ ②成果, 報い 動収穫する
- **has** 動have(持つ)の3人称単数現在 助haveの3人称単数現在《現在完了の文をつくる》
- **hat** 名(縁のある)帽子 straw hat 麦わら帽子
- **hate** 動嫌う, 憎む, (~するのを)いやがる 名憎しみ
- **have** 動①持つ, 持っている, 抱く ②(~が)ある, いる ③食べる, 飲む ④経験する, (病気に)かかる ⑤催す, 開く ⑥(人に)~させる have to ~しなければならない have to do with ~と関係がある 助《(have + 過去分詞)の形で現在完了の文をつくる》 ~した, ~したことがある, ずっと~している
- **Hawaii** 名ハワイ《米国の州》
- **he** 代彼は[が]
- **head** 名①頭 ②先頭 ③長, 指導者 動向かう, 向ける head to ~に向かう
- **health** 名健康(状態), 衛生, 保健
- **healthy** 形健康な, 健全な, 健康によい
- **hear** 動聞く, 聞こえる hear from ~から手紙[電話・返事]をもらう hear of ~について聞く I hear (that) ~だそうだ
- **heard** 動hear(聞く)の過去, 過去分詞
- **hearing** 動hear(聞く)の現在分詞 名①聞くこと, 聴取, 聴力 ②聴聞

会, ヒアリング

- **heat** 名 ①熱, 暑さ ②熱気, 熱意, 激情 poor conductor of heat 熱を伝導しない 動熱する, 暖める
- **heaven** 名 ①天国 ②天国のようなところ[状態], 楽園 ③空 ④《H-》神
- **heavy** 形 重い, 激しい, つらい
- **held** 動 hold(つかむ)の過去, 過去分詞
- **help** 動 ①助ける, 手伝う ②給仕する cannot[can't] help ~ing[but ~]~せずにはいられない help oneself 自分で取って食べる[飲む] help out(困ったときに)助ける help someone with (人)の~を手助けする 名 助け, 手伝い
- **helpful** 形 役に立つ, 参考になる
- **her** 代 ①彼女を[に] ②彼女の
- **here** 副 ①ここに[で] ②《- is[are]~》ここに~がある ③さあ, そら Here it is. はい, どうぞ。 Here we are. さあ着きました。 Here you are. はい, どうぞ。 Look here. ほら, ねえ。 名 ここ
- **hers** 代 彼女のもの
- **hesitate** 動 ためらう, ちゅうちょする
- **hey** 間 ①《呼びかけ・注意を促して》おい, ちょっと ②へえ, おや, まあ
- **hi** 間 おい, やあ
- **hid** 動 hide(隠れる)の過去, 過去分詞
- **high** 形 ①高い ②気高い, 高価な high blood pressure 高血圧症 副 ①高く ②ぜいたくに 名 高い所
- **high-level** 形 ハイレベルな, 高水準の
- **highly** 副 ①大いに, 非常に ②高度に, 高位に ③高く評価して, 高価で
- **hiking** 動 hike(ハイキングする)の現在分詞 名 ハイキング

- **hill** 名 丘, 塚
- **him** 代 彼を[に]
- **himself** 代 彼自身
- **his** 代 ①彼の ②彼のもの
- **historian** 名 歴史家
- **historically** 副 歴史的に
- **history** 名 史, 経歴
- **hit** 動 ①打つ, なぐる ②ぶつける, ぶつかる ③命中する ④(天災などが)襲う ⑤hitの過去, 過去分詞 hit on[upon] ~を思いつく 名 ①打撃 ②命中 ③大成功
- **hmm** 間 ふむ, ううむ《熟考・疑問・ためらいなどを表す》
- **hmmm** 間 ふむ, ううむ《熟考・疑問・ためらいなどを表す》
- **hobby** 名 趣味, 得意なこと
- **hold** 動 ①つかむ, 持つ, 抱く ②保つ, 持ちこたえる ③収給できる, 入れることができる ④(会などを)開く hold on to ~にしがみつく 名 ①つかむこと, 保有 ②支配[理解]力
- **hole** 名 ①穴, すき間 ②苦境, 困難 動 穴をあける, 穴に入る[入れる]
- **holiday** 名 祝祭日, 休暇 形 ①休日[休暇]の ②よそ行きの, 楽しい
- **home** 名 ①家, 自国, 故郷, 家庭 ②収容所 at home 在宅して, 気楽に, くつろいで 副 家に, 自国へ last train home 帰りの最終列車 形 家の, 家庭の, 地元の 動 ①家[本国]に帰る ②(飛行機などを)誘導する
- **homepage** 名 ホームページ
- **hometown** 名 ①生まれ故郷, 出身地 ②現在住んでいる町 形 故郷の
- **homework** 名 宿題, 予習
- **honest** 形 ①正直な, 誠実な, 心からの ②公正な, 感心な
- **hop** 動 ①(片足で)ぴょんと飛ぶ, 飛び越える, 飛び乗る ②飛行機で行く, 短い旅行をする hop in 車に乗り込む 名 ①ぴょんと飛ぶこと, 跳躍 ②ホップ《クワ科多年生の草の総称》

186

WORD LIST

- **hope** 名希望, 期待, 見込み in the hope of ～を望んで[期待して] 動望む, (～であるようにと)思う I hope (that) ～だと思う, ～だとよいと思う
- **horrible** 形恐ろしい, ひどい
- **hot** 形①暑い, 熱い ②できたての, 新しい ③からい, 強烈な, 熱中した hot spot 人気のある場所 hot spring 温泉 副①熱く ②激しく
- **hotel** 名ホテル, 旅館
- **hour** 名1時間, 時間
- **house** 名①家, 家庭 ②(特定の目的のための)建物, 小屋
- **household** 名家族, 世帯 household product 家庭用品 形家族の
- **how** 副①どうやって, どれくらい, どんなふうに ②なんて(～だろう) ③《関係副詞》～する方法 How do you like ～? ～はどう思いますか, ～はいかがですか, how to どのように～すべきか, ～する方法
- **however** 副たとえ～でも 接けれども, だが
- **huge** 形巨大な, ばく大な
- **human** 形人間の, 人の 名人間 human being 人, 人間 human destruction 人為的破壊
- **humor** 名①ユーモア ②(一時的な)機嫌 out of humor 不機嫌で, 怒って 動機嫌をとる
- **hundred** 名①100(の数字), 100人[個] ②(-s)何百, 多数 形①100の, 100人[個]の ②多数の
- **hungry** 形①空腹の, 飢えた ②渇望して ③不毛の
- **hunt** 動狩る, 狩りをする, 探し求める 名狩り, 追跡
- **hunter** 名①狩りをする人, 狩人, ハンター ②猟馬, 猟犬
- **hurry** 動急ぐ, 急がせる, あわてる 名急ぐこと, 急ぐ必要
- **hurt** 動傷つける, 痛む, 害する 名傷, けが, 苦痛, 害
- **hygiene** 名衛生(学), 清潔 hygiene hypothesis 衛生仮説
- **Hyogo** 名兵庫県
- **hypothesis** 名仮説, 仮定 hygiene hypothesis 衛生仮説

I

- **I** 代私は[が]
- **ICA** 略 International Calorie Association 国際カロリー協会
- **ice** 名①氷 ②氷菓子 動凍る, 凍らす, 氷で冷やす
- **idea** 名考え, 意見, アイデア, 計画
- **ideal** 名理想, 目標 形理想的な, 申し分ない
- **ideally** 副理想的に, 申し分なく
- **identity** 名①同一であること ②本人であること ③独自性
- **if** 接もし～ならば, たとえ～でも, ～かどうか if any もしあれば, あったとしても if at all 仮にあったとしても what if もし～だったらどうなるだろうか 名疑問, 条件, 仮定
- **illegal** 形違法な, 不法な
- **image** 名①印象, 姿 ②画像, 映像 動心に描く, 想像する
- **imagine** 動想像する, 心に思い描く
- **imitate** 動まねる, 模造する
- **immediately** 副すぐに, ～するやいなや
- **immunity** 名免疫, 免除
- **importance** 名重要性, 大切さ
- **important** 形重要な, 大切な, 有力な
- **impression** 名①印象, 感想 ②感動
- **impressive** 形印象的な, 深い感銘を与える

- **improper** 形 不適切な, 妥当でない improper behavior 不適切な行為
- **improve** 動 改善する[させる], 進歩する
- **in** 前 ①《場所・位置・所属》~(の中)に[で・の] ②《時》~(の中)に[の・で], ~後(に), ~の間(に) ③《方法・手段》~で ④~を身につけて, ~を着て ⑤~に関して, ~について ⑥《状態》~の状態で 副 へ[に], 内へ[に]
- **inappropriate** 形 不適当な, まずい
- **incident** 名 出来事, 事故, 事変, 紛争 形 ①起こりがちな ②付随する
- **include** 動 含む, 勘定に入れる
- **income** 名 収入, 所得, 収益
- **incoming** 形 入ってくる
- **increase** 動 増加[増強]する, 増やす, 増える 名 増加(量), 増大 on the increase 増加して
- **increased** 形 増大した, 増加した
- **increasing** 形 増加している, ますます増える
- **increasingly** 副 ますます, だんだん
- **indeed** 副 ①実際, 本当に ②《強意》まったく 間 本当に, まさか
- **independent** 形 独立した, 自立した
- **index** 名 ①索引 ②しるし, 現れ ③指数
- **index finger** 人差し指
- **India** 名 インド《国名》
- **indicate** 動 ①指す, 示す, (道などを)教える ②それとなく言う ③きざしがある
- **individual** 形 独立した, 個性的な, 個々の 名 個体, 個人
- **industrial** 形 工業の, 産業の
- **industry** 名 産業, 工業
- **inequality** 名 ①不平等, 不均衡 ②《-ties》起伏, (表面の)荒いこと ③(天候・温度の)変動 ④不等式
- **inexpensively** 副 安価に
- **inexperience** 名 未経験, 不慣れ
- **influence** 名 影響, 勢力 動 影響をおよぼす
- **influential** 形 影響力の大きい, 有力な
- **information** 名 ①情報, 通知, 知識 ②案内(所), 受付(係)
- **Information Technology** 情報技術, IT
- **information-rich** 形 情報の豊富な
- **information-sharing** 形 情報の共有
- **infrastructure** 名 インフラ, 社会基盤
- **ingredient** 名 成分, 原料, 材料
- **inhabitant** 名 居住者, 住民
- **initial** 形 最初の, 初めの initial work 初期の仕事 名 頭文字 動 頭文字で署名する
- **injury** 名 ①けが ②侮辱, 無礼
- **inn** 名 宿屋, 居酒屋
- **inner** 形 ①内部の ②心の中の inner ear 内なる耳
- **innocent** 形 ①無害の, 潔白な ②無邪気な, 無害の
- **insect** 名 虫, 昆虫 insect bites 虫刺されのあと insect spray 殺虫スプレー
- **inside** 名 内部, 内側 inside out 裏返しに, ひっくり返して 形 内部[内側]にある 副 内部[内側]に 前 ~の内部[内側]に
- **insist** 動 ①主張する, 断言する ②要求する
- **inspire** 動 ①奮い立たせる, 鼓舞する ②(感情などを)吹き込む ③霊感を与える
- **instance** 名 ①例 ②場合, 事実

WORD LIST

- for instance たとえば
- **instant** 形即時の,緊急の,即席の 名瞬間,寸時 in an instant 一瞬のうちに
- **instantly** 副すぐに,即座に
- **instead** 副その代わりに instead of ~の代わりに,~をしないで
- **instruct** 動①教える,教育する ②指図[命令]する
- **insult** 動侮辱する,ばかにする 名侮辱,無礼な言動
- **insulting** 形侮辱的な,無礼な
- **intelligence** 名①知能 ②情報
- **intelligent** 形頭のよい,聡明な
- **intend** 動《-to~》~しようと思う,~するつもりである
- **interaction** 名相互作用,相互の影響,対話 social interaction 社会的交流
- **interest** 名①興味,関心 ②利害(関係),利益 ③利子,利息 動興味を起こさせる
- **interested** 動 interest(興味を起こさせる)の過去,過去分詞 形興味を持った,関心のある
- **interesting** 動 interest(興味を起こさせる)の現在分詞 形おもしろい,興味を起こさせる
- **international** 形国際(間)の
- **International Calorie Association** 国際カロリー協会
- **International Year of the Volunteer** ボランティア国際年
- **Internet** 名インターネット
- **interpreter** 名解説者,通訳
- **interrupt** 動さえぎる,妨害する,口をはさむ
- **intersection** 名交差点
- **interview** 名会見,面接 動会見[面接]する
- **into** 前①《動作・運動の方向》~の中へ[に] ②《変化》~に[へ]
- **introduce** 動紹介する,採り入れる,導入する
- **investigate** 動研究する,調査する,捜査する
- **invite** 動①招待する,招く ②勧める,誘う ③~をもたらす
- **involve** 動①含む,伴う ②巻き込む,かかわらせる
- **iron** 名①鉄,鉄製のもの ②アイロン 形鉄の,鉄製の 動アイロンをかける
- **is** 動 be(~である)の3人称単数現在
- **Israel** 名イスラエル《国名》
- **issue** 名①問題,論点 ②発行物 ③出口,流出 at issue 論争中の,(意見が)一致しない 動①(~から)出る,生じる ②発行する
- **it** 代①それは[が],それを[に] ②《天候・日時・距離・寒暖などを示す》
- **Italian** 形イタリア(人・語)の 名①イタリア人 ②イタリア語
- **Italy** 名イタリア《国名》
- **item** 名①項目,品目 ②(新聞などの)記事
- **its** 代それの,あれの
- **itself** 代それ自体,それ自身

J

- **Jamas** 名ジャマス《都市名》
- **Japan** 名日本《国名》
- **Japan National Tourist Organization** 国際観光振興会
- **Japanese** 形日本(人・語)の Japanese cuisine 日本料理 名①日本人 ②日本語
- **Jay** 名ジェイ《人名》
- **jealous** 形嫉妬して,嫉妬深い,うらやんで
- **Jean-Jacques Rousseau** ジ

ヤン＝ジャック・ルソー《スイス生まれの哲学者、思想家、1712-1778》
- **jeans** 名 ジーンズ、ジーパン
- **Jemison** 名 メイ・ジェミソン《医師、大学教授、元宇宙飛行士》
- **Jerry** 名 ジェリー《人名》
- **Jin Ah** ジン・アー《人名》
- **JNTO** 略 Japan National Tourist Organization 国際観光振興会
- **job** 名 仕事、職 do [make] a good job うまくやってのける Good job! よくやった。
- **job search** 就職活動
- **Joe** 名 ジョー《人名》
- **Johann Heinrich Pestalozzi** ヨハン・ハインリッヒ・ペスタロッチ《スイスの教育実践家、1746-1827》
- **Johnson** 名 ジョンソン《人名》
- **join** 動 ①一緒になる、参加する ②連結［結合］する、つなぐ join in 加わる、参加する 名 結合
- **joke** 名 冗談、ジョーク 動 冗談を言う、ふざける、からかう
- **Jonestown** 名 ジョーンズタウン《都市名》
- **Jordan** 名 ジョーダン《人名》
- **journal** 名 雑誌、機関紙、日誌
- **joy** 名 喜び、楽しみ
- **judge** 動 判決を下す、裁く、判断する、評価する 名 裁判官、判事、審査員
- **judgment** 名 ①判断、意見 ②裁判、判決
- **juice** 名 ジュース、液、汁
- **jump** 動 ①跳ぶ、跳躍する、飛び越える、飛びかかる ②(～を)熱心にやり始める 名 ①跳躍 ②急騰、急転
- **junior** 形 年少の、年下の 名 年少者、年下の者
- **junior high school** 中学校
- **just** 形 正しい、もっともな、当然な 副 ①まさに、ちょうど、(～した)ばかり ②ほんの、単に、ただ～だけ ③

ちょっと

K

- **Kagoshima** 名 鹿児島《県名》
- **Kaori** 名 佳織《人名》
- **Kate** 名 ケイト《人名》
- **kcal** 略 kilocalorie キロカロリー《熱量の単位》
- **keep** 動 ①とっておく、保つ、続ける ②(～を…に)しておく ③飼う、養う ④経営する ⑤守る keep control over ～を管理下に置いておく keep off ～を避ける keep on ～[～ing] ～し続ける、繰り返し～する keep out (場所に)入らせない、締め出す keep to ～から離れない、～を守る keep up 続ける、続く、維持する、(遅れないで)ついていく
- **keeper** 名 ①番人、看守 ②保護者 record keeper 記録係
- **kept** 動 keep (とっておく)の過去、過去分詞
- **Kevin** 名 ケヴィン《人名》
- **keyword** 名 キーワード、鍵となる語
- **kick** 動 ける、キックする kick off 始める、キックオフする 名 けること
- **kid** 名 子ども
- **kill** 動 殺す、消す、枯らす 名 殺すこと
- **kilogram** 名 キログラム《重量の単位》
- **kilometer** 名 キロメートル《長さの単位》 square kilometer 平方キロメートル
- **Kim Higgins** キム・ヒギンズ《人名》
- **kimono** 名 着物 in kimono 着物を着た
- **kind** 形 親切な、優しい be kind enough to 親切にも～する 名 種類 kind of (～) ある程度、いくらか、～

WORD LIST

のような物[人]
- **king** 名王, 国王
- **Kinkakuji** 名金閣寺
- **Kishan Santha** キシャン・サンサ《人名》
- **kiss** 名キス 動キスする
- **kitten** 名子猫
- **kl** 略 kiloliter キロリットル《容量の単位》
- **knew** 動 know（知っている）の過去
- **knock** 動ノックする, たたく, ぶつける 名打つこと, 戸をたたくこと［音］
- **know** 動(1)知っている, 知る, (〜が)わかる, 理解している (2)知り合いである **get to know** 知るようになる, 知り合う **know better (than 〜)** (〜より)もっと分別がある **Who knows?** 誰にわかるだろうか, 誰にもわからない, **you know** ご存知のとおり, そうでしょう
- **knowledge** 名知識, 理解, 学問
- **known** 動 know（知っている）の過去分詞 形知られた
- **Korea** 名朝鮮, 韓国［国名］
- **Korean** 形韓国（人・語）の, 朝鮮（人・語）の 名(1)韓国［朝鮮］人 (2)韓国［朝鮮］語
- **Kyoto** 名京都

L

- **L-shaped** 形 L字型の
- **label** 名標札, ラベル
- **labor** 名労働, 骨折り 動(1)働く, 努力する, 骨折る (2)苦しむ, 悩む
- **lack** 動不足している, 欠けている **lack for** 〜がなくて困る 名不足, 欠乏
- **lake** 名湖, 湖水, 池
- **Lancaster** 名ランカスター《イギリスの都市》
- **land** 名(1)陸地, 土地 (2)国, 領域 動上陸する, 着地する
- **lane** 名車線, 小道
- **language** 名言語, 言葉, 国語, 〜語, 専門語 **pick up the language** 言葉を覚える **sign language** 手話
- **large** 形(1)大きい, 広い (2)大勢の, 多量の 副(1)大きく (2)自慢して
- **last** 形(1)《the 〜》最後の (2)この前の, 先〜 (3)最新の **at the last second** 最後の最後で **last train home** 帰りの最終列車 **the last time**《接続詞的に》この前〜したとき **until the last minute** 最後まで 副(1)最後に (2)この前 名《the 〜》最後（のもの）, 終わり **at last** ついに 動続く, 持ちこたえる
- **late** 形(1)遅い, 後期の (2)最近の (3)《the 〜》故〜 副(1)遅れて, 遅く (2)最近まで, 以前
- **latter** 形後の, 末の, 後者の (2)《the 〜》後者《代名詞的に用いる》
- **laugh** 動笑う 名笑い（声）
- **laughter** 名笑い（声）
- **law** 名(1)法, 法律 (2)弁護士業, 訴訟 **rainforest protection laws** 熱帯雨林保護法
- **lay** 動(1)置く, 横たえる, 敷く (2)整える (3)卵を産む (4)lie（横たわる）の過去 **lay off** レイオフする, 一時解雇する
- **layer** 名層, 重ね 動層になる［する］
- **lead** 動(1)導く, 案内する (2)《生活を》送る 名(1)鉛 (2)先導, 指導 **lead over** 〜に対する優位
- **leader** 名指導者, リーダー
- **leadership** 名指揮, リーダーシップ
- **leading** 動 lead（導く）の現在分詞 形主要な, 指導的な, 先頭の
- **learn** 動学ぶ, 習う, 教わる, 知識［経験］を得る

Readings from the National Center Test for English

- **learner** 名学習者, 初心者
- **learning** 動learn (学ぶ) の現在分詞 名学問, 学習, 学識
- **least** 形いちばん小さい, 最も少ない 副いちばん小さく, 最も少なく 名最小, 最少 at least 少なくとも
- **leave** 動①出発する, 去る ②残す, 置き忘れる ③(~を…の) ままにしておく ④ゆだねる leave ~ alone ~をそっとしておく leave behind あとにする 名①休暇 ②許可 ③別れ
- **leaves** 名leaf (葉) の複数 動leave (出発する) の3人称単数現在
- **led** 動lead (導く) の過去, 過去分詞
- **left** 名《the-》左, 左側 形左の, 左側の 副左に, 左側に 動leave (する) の過去, 過去分詞 left out 仲間はずれになる
- **leisure** 名余暇 at leisure 暇で, ゆっくり at one's leisure 暇な時に 形余暇の
- **lent** 動lend (貸す) の過去, 過去分詞
- **less** 形より小さい [少ない] 副~より少なく, ~ほどでなく less and less だんだん少なく~, ますます~でなく no less than ~と同じだけの, ~も同然 not less than ~以下ではなく, ~にまさるとも劣らない 名より少ない数 [量・額]
- **lesson** 名①授業, 学科, 課, けいこ ②教訓, 戒め
- **let** 動 (人に~) させる, (~するのを) 許す, (~をある状態に) する Let me see. ええと。
- **let's** let us の短縮形
- **letter** 名①手紙 ②文字 ③文学, 文筆業
- **level** 名①水平, 平面 ②水準 形①水平の, 平たい ②同等 [同位] の 動①水平にする ②平等にする
- **life** 名①生命, 生物 ②一生, 生涯, 人生 ③生活, 暮らし, 世の中

- **lifestyle** 名生活様式, ライフスタイル
- **lift** 動①持ち上げる, 上がる ②取り除く, 撤廃する 名①持ち上げること ②エレベーター, リフト
- **light** 名光, 明かり 動火をつける, 照らす, 明るくする 形①明るい ②(色が) 薄い, 淡い ③軽い, 容易な 副軽く, 容易に
- **like** 動好む, 好きである would like ~がほしい would like to ~したいと思う Would you like ~? ~はいかが feel like ~のように感じる, ~がほしい look like ~のように見える, ~に似ている 形似ている, ~のような 接あたかも~のように 名好きなもの ②《the [one's] –》同じようなもの [人]
- **likely** 形①ありそうな, (~) しそうな ②適当な 副たぶん, おそらく
- **limit** 名限界, 《-s》範囲, 境界 動制限 [限定] する
- **limitation** 名制限, 限度
- **limited** 動limit (制限する) の過去, 過去分詞 形限られた, 限定の
- **line** 名①線, 糸, 電話線 ②(字の) 行 ③列, (電車の) ~線 動①線を引く ②整列する
- **linear** 形①直線の, 線状の ②一次元の
- **lip** 名唇, 《-s》口
- **liquid** 名液体 形①液体 (状) の, 流動する ②流ちょうな ③澄んだ ④不安定な
- **list** 名名簿, 目録, 一覧表 動名簿 [目録] に記入する
- **listen** 動《–to ~》~を聞く, ~に耳を傾ける
- **little** 形①小さい, 幼い ②少しの, 短い ③ほとんど~ない, 《a–》少しはある 名少し (しか), 少量 little by little 少しずつ 副全然~ない, 《a–》少しはある

192

Word List

- **live** 動住む, 暮らす, 生きている those living in Tokyo 東京に住む人々 形①生きている, 生きた ②ライブの, 実況の 副生で, ライブで
- **living environment** 生活環境
- **local** 形①地方の, ある場所[土地]の, 部分的な ②各駅停車の local product 地場産品 名ある特定の地方のもの
- **locally** 副①ある特定の場所[地方]で, 現地的に ②近くで, このあたりで
- **locate** 動置く, 居住する[させる]
- **location** 名位置, 場所
- **lock** 名錠(前) 動錠をドロす, 閉じ込める, 動けなくする
- **logo** 名ロゴ, 文字, 意匠文字
- **Lomita** 名ロミタ《都市名》
- **loneliness** 名孤独
- **long** 形①長い, 長期の ②《長さ・距離・時間などを示す語句を伴って》〜の長さ[距離・時間]の 副長い間, ずっと no longer もはや〜でない[〜しない] not 〜 any longer もはや〜でない[〜しない] so [as] long as 〜する限りは 名長い期間 before long 間もなく, やがて 動切望する, 思い焦がれる
- **long-established** 形長い歴史を持つ, 長い伝統のある
- **long-term** 形長期の
- **look** 動①見る ②(〜に)見える, (〜の)顔つきをする ③注意する ④《間投詞のように》ほら, ねえ look after 〜の世話をする, 〜に気をつける look down on 〜を見下す look down upon 見下ろす look for 〜を探す look over into 〜の方を見る look over 〜を見渡す look up (言葉を)調べる Take a look. ちょっと見てごらん。 名①一見, 目つき ②外観, 外見, 様子
- **loop** 動①輪にする ②輪で囲む 名ループ, 輪, 輪状のもの

- **loose** 形自由な, ゆるんだ, あいまいな 動ほどく, 解き放つ
- **lose** 動①失う, 迷う, 忘れる ②負ける, 失敗する lose track of time どのくらい時間がたったか分からなくなる
- **loss** 名①損失(額・物), 損害, 浪費 ②失敗, 敗北 at a loss 途方に暮れて
- **lost** 動 lose (失う)の過去, 過去分詞 形①失った, 負けた ②道に迷った, 困った ③没頭している
- **lot** 名①くじ, 運 ②地所, 区画 ③たくさん, たいへん,《a - of 〜 / -s of 〜》たくさんの〜 ④やつ, 連中
- **loud** 形大声の, 騒がしい 副大声に[で]
- **Louis XIV** ルイ14世《フランス王, 1638-1715》
- **Louvre Museum** ルーブル美術館《フランスの国立美術館》
- **love** 名愛, 愛情, 思いやり 動愛する, 恋する, 大好きである
- **low** 形①低い, 弱い ②低級の, 劣等な 副低く 名①低い水準[点] ②低速ギア
- **low-fat** 形低脂肪の
- **luckily** 副運よく, 幸いにも
- **lucky** 形幸運な, 運のよい, 縁起のよい
- **lunch** 名昼食, ランチ, 軽食
- **lung** 名肺
- **lying** 動 lie (うそをつく・横たわる)の現在分詞 形①うそをつく, 虚偽の ②横になっている 名①うそをつくこと, 虚言, 虚偽 ②横たわること

M

- **mad** 形①気の狂った ②逆上した, 理性をなくした ③ばかげた ④(〜に)熱狂[熱中]して, 夢中の go mad 発狂する

Readings from the National Center Test for English

- **made** 動 make（作る）の過去, 過去分詞 形 作った, 作られた
- **Madoka** 名 まどか《人名》
- **Mae Jemison** メイ・ジェミソン《医師, 大学教授, 元宇宙飛行士》
- **magazine** 名 ①雑誌, 定期刊行物 ②弾倉
- **magnificent** 形 壮大な, 壮麗な, すばらしい
- **Maiko** 名 麻衣子《人名》
- **Mailman Jack** 郵便配達人ジャック
- **mail-order catalog** 通販カタログ
- **main** 形 主な, 主要な
- **maintain** 動 ①維持する ②養う
- **major** 形 ①大きいほうの, 主な, 一流の ②年長〔古参〕の 名 ①陸軍少佐 ②専攻科目 動 専攻する　major in ~ を専攻する
- **majority** 名 ①大多数, 大部分 ②過半数
- **make** 動 ①作る, 得る ②行う, (~になる) ③(~を…に) ④(~を…)させる　make do with ~で間に合わせる　make it 到達する, 成功する　make out 認識する, 見分ける　make ~ out of … ~を…から作る　make up ~を構成〔形成〕する　make up for ~の埋め合わせをする
- **male** 形 男の, 雄の 名 男, 雄
- **mall** 名 ショッピングモール
- **man** 名 男性, 人, 人類
- **mandatory** 形 ①強制的な, 義務的な ②命令の
- **manner** 名 ①方法, やり方 ②態度, 様子 ③(-s)行儀, 作法, 生活様式
- **manufacturing** 名 製造業 形 製造業の
- **many** 形 多数の, たくさんの 代 多数(の人・物)
- **map** 名 地図 動 ①地図を作る ②計画を立てる

- **Maria** 名 マリア《人名》
- **mark** 名 ①印, 記号, 跡 ②点数 ③特色 動 ①印〔記号〕をつける ②採点する ③目立たせる
- **market** 名 市場, マーケット, 取引, 需要 動 市場に出す
- **martial art** 武術, マーシャル・アート
- **massive** 形 ①巨大な, 大量の ②堂々とした
- **master** 名 主人, 雇い主, 師, 名匠 動 ①習得する ②~の主となる
- **match** 名 ①試合, 勝負 ②相手, 釣り合うもの ③マッチ（棒）動 ①(~を…と)勝負させる ②調和する, 釣り合う　match up to ~と合致〔匹敵〕する
- **mate** 名 仲間, 連れ 動 ①交尾する〔させる〕 ②仲間になる, 結婚する
- **material** 形 ①物質の, 肉体的な ②不可欠な, 重要な 名 材料, 原料
- **mathematics** 名 数学
- **matter** 名 物, 事, 事件, 問題　as a matter of course 当然のこと　as a matter of fact 実際は　no matter how どんなに~であろうとも 動《主に疑問文・否定文で》重要である
- **may** 助 ①~かもしれない ②~してもよい, ~できる　May I ~? ~してもよいですか 名 (M-) 5月
- **maybe** 副 たぶん, おそらく
- **McDonald** 名 マクドナルド《人名》
- **me** 代 私を〔に〕
- **meal** 名 ①食事 ②ひいた粉, あらびき粉
- **mean** 動 ①意味する ②(~のつもりで)言う, 意図する ③~するつもりである　I mean つまり, そうではなく 形 ①卑怯な, けちな, 卑しい ②中間の 名 中間, 中位
- **meaning** 動 mean（意味する）の現在分詞 名 意味, 意義 形 意味ありげな

WORD LIST

- **meant** 動 mean（意味する）の過去, 過去分詞
- **measure** 動 ①測る, (~の)寸法がある ②評価する 名 ①寸法, 測定, 計量, 単位 ②程度, 基準
- **medical** 形 ①医学の ②内科の medical doctor 医師 名 健康診断, 身体検査
- **medicinal** 形 薬効のある
- **medicine** 名 ①薬 ②医学, 内科
- **medieval** 形 中世の, 中世風の
- **meet** 動 ①会う, 知り合いになる ②合流する, 交わる ③《条件などに》達する, 合う meet with ~に出会う
- **meeting** 動 meet（会う）の現在分詞 名 ①集まり, ミーティング, 面会 ②競技会
- **melody** 名 メロディー, 旋律
- **member** 名 一員, メンバー
- **memorize** 動 暗記する, 記憶する
- **memory** 名 ①記憶（力）, 思い出 ②（コンピュータの）メモリ, 記憶装置
- **men** 名 man（男性）の複数
- **mental** 形 ①心の, 精神の ②知能［知性］の
- **mention** 動 (~について)述べる, 言及する Don't mention it. どういたしまして。 名 言及, 陳述
- **merchant** 名 商人, 貿易商
- **message** 名 伝言, (作品などに込められた)メッセージ get the message (人の)真意をつかむ 動 メッセージで送る, 伝える
- **met** 動 meet（会う）の過去, 過去分詞
- **meter** 名 ①メートル《長さの単位》②計量器, 計量する人
- **method** 名 ①方法, 手段 ②秩序, 体系
- **Mexico** 名 メキシコ《国名》
- **middle** 名 中間, 最中 形 中間の, 中央の
- **middle finger** 中指
- **middle-class** 形 中流階級の
- **might** 助 《may の過去》①~かもしれない ②~してもよい, ~できる 名 力, 権力
- **Mika** 名 美加《人名》
- **mile** 名 ①マイル《長さの単位。1,609m》②《-s》かなりの距離
- **milk** 名 牛乳, ミルク 動 乳をしぼる
- **million** 名 ①100万 ②《-s》数百万, 多数 Thanks a million. ありがとう。形 ①100万の ②多数の
- **mind** 名 ①心, 精神, 考え ②知性 make up one's mind 決心する 動 ①気にする, いやがる ②気をつける, 用心する Never mind. 心配するな。
- **mine** 代 私のもの 名 鉱山 動 採掘する, 坑道を掘る
- **mining company** 炭鉱会社
- **ministry** 名 ①《M-》内閣, 省庁 ②大臣の職務 ③牧師の職務
- **minute** 名 ①(時間の)分 ②ちょっとの間 Just [Wait] a minute. ちょっと待って。 until the last minute 最後まで 形 ごく小さい, 細心の
- **miss** 動 ①失敗する, 免れる, ~を見逃す, (目標を)はずす ②(~が)ないのに気づく, (人が)いなくてさびしく思う ③(~が)はずれ, 失敗 ②《M-》《女性に対して》~さん, ~先生
- **mission** 名 ①使命, 任務 ②使節団, 代表団, 派遣団 ③伝道, 布教
- **mmm** 間 ウーン
- **model** 名 ①模型, 設計図 ②模範 role model 模範になる人 形 模範の, 典型的な 動 (~をもとにして)作る, 模型を作る
- **moderator** 名 司会
- **modern** 形 現代［近代］の, 現代的な, 最近の modern architecture 現代建築 名 現代［近代］人

- **Mom** 名 お母さん, ママ《主に呼びかけに用いる》
- **moment** 名 ①瞬間, ちょっとの間 ②(特定の)時, 時期 **at any moment** いつ何時, 今にも **at the moment** 今は **in a moment** ただちに
- **monday** 名 月曜日
- **Money** 名 金, 通貨
- **Monica Molina** モニカ・モリーナ《人名》
- **monolingual** 名形 単一言語(の)
- **month** 名 月, 1ヵ月
- **Moon Suk** ムーン・サク《人名》
- **more** 形 ①もっと多くの ②それ以上の, 余分の 副 もっと, さらに多く, いっそう **more and more** ますます **more or less** 多少, 多かれ少なかれ **no more** もう〜ない **no more than** たった〜, ほんの〜 **not 〜 any more** [これ以上]〜ない **once more** もう一度 **the more 〜, the more …** 〜すればするほどますます… 代 もっと多くの物[人]
- **moreover** 副 その上, さらに
- **morning** 名 朝, 午前
- **mosquito** 名 カ(蚊)
- **most** 形 ①最も多い ②たいていの, 大部分の 代 ①大部分, ほとんど ②最多数, 最大限 **at (the) most** せいぜい, 多くても **make the most of** 〜を最大限利用する 副 最も(多く) **most of all** とりわけ, 中でも
- **mostly** 副 主として, 多くは, ほとんど
- **mother** 名 母, 母親
- **mountain** 名 ①山 ②《the 〜 M-s》〜山脈 ③山のようなもの, 多量
- **move** 動 ①動く, 動かす ②感動させる ③引っ越す, 移動する 名 ①動き, 運動 ②転居, 移動
- **movement** 名 ①動き, 運動 ②《-s》行動 ③引っ越し ④変動
- **movie** 名 映画, 映画館

- **Mr.** 《男性に対して。Mrとも》〜さん, 〜氏, 〜先生
- **Ms.** 《女性に対して。Msとも》〜さん, 〜先生
- **Mt. Fuji** 富士山
- **much** 形 (量・程度が)多くの, 多量の **as much 〜 as** …と同じだけの〜 副 ①とても, たいへん ②《比較級・最上級を修飾して》ずっと, はるかに 名 多量, たくさん, 重要なもの **as much as** 〜と同じだけ
- **muddy** 形 泥だらけの, ぬかるみの 動 泥まみれにする, 濁らせる
- **muscle** 名 筋肉, 腕力 動 強引に押し進む, 力ずくで進む
- **museum** 名 博物館, 美術館
- **mushroom** 名 ①キノコ, マッシュルーム ②キノコ状のもの 動 ①(キノコのように)急速に生じる, キノコ形になる ②キノコ狩りをする
- **music** 名 音楽, 楽曲
- **musical** 形 音楽の 名 ミュージカル
- **musician** 名 音楽家
- **must** 助 ①〜しなければならない ②〜に違いない 名 絶対に必要なこと[もの]
- **my** 代 私の
- **myself** 代 私自身

N

- **nail** 名 ①爪 ②くぎ, びょう 動 くぎを打つ, くぎづけにする
- **name** 名 ①名前 ②名声 ③《-s》悪口 **by name** 名前で, 名前だけは **call 〜 names** 〜の悪口を言う 動 ①名前をつける ②名指しする **name after [for]** 〜の名をとって命名する
- **Naomi** 名 奈緒美《人名》
- **narrow** 形 ①狭い ②限られた 動 狭くなる[する]

Word List

- **nasty** 形 ①不快な ②意地の悪い ③荒れ模様の
- **nation** 名 国, 国家, 《the -》国民
- **national** 形 国家[国民]の, 全国の
- **National Championships** 全国選手権
- **nation-states** 名 国民国家
- **native** 形 ①出生(地)の, 自国の ②(~に)固有の, 生まれつきの, 天然の native tribes 先住民 名 (ある土地に)生まれた人
- **Natsumi** 名 夏美《人名》
- **natural** 形 ①自然の, 天然の ②生まれつきの, 天性の ③当然な
- **naturally** 副 生まれつき, 自然に, 当然
- **nature** 名 ①自然(界) ②天性, 性質 ③自然のまま, 実物 ④本質 by nature 生まれつき
- **near** 前 ~の近くに, ~のそばに 形 近い, 親しい 副 近くに, 親密で
- **nearly** 副 ①近くに, 親しく ②ほとんど, あやうく
- **neat** 形 きちんとした, きれいな
- **necessarily** 副 ①必ず, 必然的に, やむを得ず ②《not -》必ずしも~でない
- **necessary** 形 必要な, 必然の if necessary もし必要ならば 名 《-s》必要品, 必需品
- **need** 動 (~を)必要とする, 必要である 助 ~する必要がある 名 ①必要(性), 《-s》必要なもの ②まさかの時 in need of 必要で, 困って
- **negative** 形 ①否定的な, 消極的な ②負の, マイナスの, (写真が)ネガの negative aspect マイナスの側面 名 ①否定, 反対 ②ネガ, 陰画, 負数, マイナス
- **negatively** 副 消極的に
- **neighbor** 名 隣人, 隣り合うもの
- **nerve** 名 ①神経 ②気力, 精力 ③《-s》神経過敏, 臆病, 憂うつ
- **nervous** 形 ①神経の ②神経質な, おどおどした
- **net** 名 ①網, 網状のもの ②わな ③正味, 純益 形 正味の, 純益の 動 ①網でつかまえる ②純益を上げる
- **never** 副 決して[少しも]~ない, 一度も[二度と]~ない
- **new** 形 ①新しい, 新規の ②新鮮な, できたての What's new? お変わりありませんか.
- **news** 名 報道, ニュース, 便り, 知らせ
- **newspaper** 名 新聞(紙)
- **next** 形 ①次の, 翌~ ②隣の 副 ①次に ②隣に next to ~の隣の, ~の次に next to each other 隣同士に 代 次の人[もの]
- **next-door** 形 隣の, 隣に住む
- **nice** 形 すてきな, よい, きれいな, 親切な Nice to meet you. お会いできてうれしい.
- **niece** 名 めい(姪)
- **night** 名 夜, 晩
- **nine** 名 9(の数字), 9人[個] nine out of ten 9割がた 形 9の, 9人[個]の
- **nineteenth** 名 《通例the -》第19番目(の人[物]), 19日 形 《通例the -》第19番目の
- **no** 副 ①いいえ, いや ②少しも~ない 形 ~がない, 少しも~ない, ~どころでない, ~禁止 名 否定, 拒否
- **nobody** 代 誰も[1人も]~ない 名 とるに足らない人
- **none** 代 (~の)何も[誰も・少しも]…ない
- **non-sweetened** 形 甘みの入っていない
- **Norstar** 名 ノースター《都市名》
- **north** 名 《the -》北, 北部 形 北の, 北からの 副 北へ[に], 北から
- **northeast** 名 北東, 北東部 形 北東の, 北東部の 副 北東に[へ]

- **northwest** 名北西(部), 形北西の, 北西向きの 副北西へ, 北西から
- **not** 副~でない, ~しない not (~) at all まったく(~で)ない not ~ but … ~ではなくて… not yet まだ~してない
- **note** 名 ①メモ, 覚え書き ②注釈 ③注意, 注目 ④手形 動①書き留める ②注意[注目]する
- **nothing** 代何も~ない[しない] for nothing ただで, 無料で, むだに have nothing to do with ~と何の関係もない nothing but ただ~だけ, ~にすぎない, ~のほかは何も~ない
- **notice** 名 ①注意 ②通知 ③公告 動 ①気づく, 認める ②通告する
- **now** 副 ①今(では), 現在 ②今すぐ ③では, さて right now 今すぐに, たった今 名今, 現在 by now 今のところ for now 当分の間, 当面は from now on 今後 形今の, 現在の
- **nowadays** 副このごろは, 現在では
- **number** 名 ①数, 数字, 番号 ②~号, ~番 ③《-s》多数 a number of いくつかの~, 多くの~ 動番号をつける, 数える
- **nurse** 名 ①看護師[人] ②乳母 動 ①看病する ②あやす

O

- **object** 名 ①物, 事物 ②目的物, 対象 動反対する, 異議を唱える
- **observation** 名観察(力), 注目 observation deck 展望台
- **obstacle** 名障害(物), じゃま(な物)
- **obtain** 動 ①得る, 獲得する ②一般に通用している
- **obviously** 副明らかに, はっきりと
- **occupation** 名 ①職業, 仕事, 就業 ②占有, 居住, 占領
- **occupational** 形職業上の, 職務柄の
- **Occupational Psychology Association** 職業心理協会
- **occur** 動(事が)起こる, 生じる, (考えなどが)浮かぶ
- **o'clock** 副~時
- **of** 前 ①《所有・所属・部分》~の, ~に属する ②《性質・特徴・材料》~の, ~製の ③《部分》~のうち ④《分離・除去》~から
- **off** 副 ①離れて ②はずれて ③止まって ④休んで time off 仕事を休んだ時間, 休暇 形 ①離れて ②季節はずれの ③休みの 前~を離れて, ~をはずれて, (値段が)~引きの
- **offend** 動 ①感情を害する ②罪を犯す, 反する
- **offensive** 形 ①いやな, いらいらさせる ②攻撃的な 名攻撃態勢, 攻撃
- **offer** 動申し出る, 申し込む, 提供する 名提案, 提供
- **office** 名 ①会社, 事務所, 職場, 役所, 局 ②官職, 地位, 役
- **official** 形 ①公式の, 正式の ②職務上の, 公の 名公務員, 役人, 職員
- **often** 副しばしば, たびたび
- **oh** 間ああ, おや, まあ
- **oil-producing** 形石油を産出する
- **OK** 形《許可・同意・満足などを表して。O.K.とも》よろしい, 正しい 名許可, 承認 動オーケー[承認]する
- **Okay** 形《許可, 同意, 満足などを表して》よろしい, 正しい 名許可, 承認 動オーケー[承認]する
- **old** 形 ①年取った, 老いた ②~歳の ③古い, 昔の 名昔, 老人
- **old saying** 古いことわざ
- **Olympic** 名オリンピック
- **omit** 動除外する, 怠る

WORD LIST

- **on** 前①《場所・接触》～(の上)に ②《日・時》～に,～と同時に,～のすぐ後で ③《関係・従事》～に関して,～について,～して 副①身につけて,上に ②前へ,続けて

- **once** 副①一度,1回 ②かつて once in a while たまに,時々 once upon a time 昔々 once 名一度,1回 all at once 突然 at once すぐに,同時に 接いったん～すると

- **one** 名①(の数字),1人[個] one by one 1つずつ,1人ずつ 形①1の,1人[個]の ②《the -》唯一の one day ある日 代①(一般の)人,ある物 ②一方,片方 ③～なもの

- **on-line** 名オンライン 形オンラインの

- **only** 形唯一の 副①単に,～にすぎない,ただ～だけ ②やっと if only ～でありさえすれば not only ～ but (also) ～だけでなく…もまた 接ただし,だがしかし

- **onto** 前～の上へ[に]

- **OPA** 略 Occupational Psychology Association 職業心理学協会

- **open** 形①開いた,広々とした ②公開された 動①開く,始まる ②広がる,広げる ③打ち明ける open up 心を開く

- **operator** 名オペレーター,交換手,操作する人

- **opinion** 名意見,見識,世論,評判

- **opportunity** 名好機,適当な時期[状況]

- **oppose** 動反対する,敵対する

- **opposite** 形反対の,向こう側の 前～の向こう側に 名反対の人[物]

- **option** 名選択(の余地),選択可能物,選択権

- **or** 接①～か…,または ②さもないと ③すなわち,言い換えると

- **orange-pink** 形オレンジピンクの

- **order** 名①順序 ②整理,整頓 ③命令,注文(品) in order きちんと(整理されて),順序正しく in order to ～するために,～しようと 動①(～するよう)命じる,注文する ②整頓する,整理する

- **ordinary** 形①普通の,通常の ②並の,平凡な

- **organization** 名①組織(化),編成,団体,機関 ②有機体,生物

- **organize** 動組織する

- **organizer** 名主催者

- **original** 形①始めの,元の,本来の ②独創的な 名原型,原文

- **originally** 副①元は,元来 ②独創的に

- **other** 形①ほかの,異なった ②(2つのうち)もう一方の,(3つ以上のうち)残りの every other 1つおきの～ on the other hand 一方 the other day 先日 代①ほかの人[物] ②《the -》残りの1つ 副そうでなく,別に

- **ouch** 間痛い！

- **ought** 助《- to ～》当然～すべきである,きっと～するはずである

- **our** 代私たちの

- **out** 副①外へ[に],不在で,離れて ②世に出て ③消えて ④すっかり get out of control 手のつけられない状態になる out of ～の外に,～から,(危険など)を脱して out of date 時代遅れの,古くさい 形①外の,遠く離れた ②公表された 前～から外へ[に] 動①追い出す ②露見する ③(スポーツで)アウトにする

- **outdoor** 形戸外の outdoor environment 屋外環境

- **outline** 名①外形,輪郭 ②概略

- **outsider** 名よそ者,部外者,門外漢

- **over** 前①～の上の[に],～を一面に覆って ②～を越えて,～以上に,～よりまさって ③～の向こう側の[に] ④～の間 副①上に,一面に,ずっと ②終わって,すんで over and over (again) 何度も繰り返して

- **overall** 形 総体的な, 全面的な 副 全般的に見れば 名 オーバーオール, 作業着
- **overdo** 動 やりすぎる, 使いすぎる
- **overeating** 名 過食, 食べ過ぎ
- **overflow** 動 氾濫する, あふれる 名 氾濫, 流出, 過剰
- **overly** 副 過度に
- **overseas** 形 海外の, 外国の 副 海外へ 名 国外
- **overweight** 形 太り過ぎの, 重量超過の
- **owe** 動 ①(~を)負う, (~を人の)お陰とする ②(金を)借りている, (人に対して~の)義務がある
- **Owen** 名 オーエン《人名》
- **own** 形 自身の 動 持っている, 所有する
- **owner** 名 持ち主, オーナー

P

- **Pacific** 形 ①平和な, 穏やかな ②《P-》太平洋の 名 《the P-》太平洋
- **pack** 名 ①包み, 荷物 ②群れ, 一組 動 荷造りする, 詰め込む **pack off** 急いで行ってしまう, どんどん行かせる, 首にする **pack up** 荷物をまとめる, 故障する, 放棄する
- **package** 名 包み, 小包, パッケージ 動 包装する, 荷造りする
- **package tour** パックツアー
- **packaged** 形 パッケージ化された
- **page** 名 ①ページ ②(ホテルなどの)ボーイ 動 (ボーイや放送で)呼び出す
- **paid** 動 pay(払う)の過去, 過去分詞 形 有給の, 支払い済みの **paid vacation** 有給休暇, 年休
- **pain** 名 ①痛み, 苦悩 ②《-s》骨折り, 苦労 動 苦痛を与える, 痛む
- **painful** 形 ①痛い, 苦しい, 痛ましい ②骨の折れる, 困難な
- **pale** 形 ①(顔色・人が)青ざめた, 青白い ②(色が)薄い, (光が)薄暗い 動 ①青ざめる, 青ざめさせる ②淡くなる[する], 色あせる
- **pan** 名 平なべ, フライパン
- **panelist** 名 パネリスト(パネルディスカッションに参加して討論する人)
- **pants** 名 ズボン, スラックス
- **paper** 名 ①紙 ②新聞, 論文, 答案 ③《-s》書類 ④紙幣, 手形
- **parent** 名 親, 《-s》両親
- **Paris** 名 パリ《フランスの首都》
- **park** 名 ①公園, 広場 ②駐車場 動 駐車する
- **parking** 動 park(駐車する)の現在分詞 名 駐車(場)
- **part** 名 ①部分, 割合 ②役目 **play a part** 役目を果たす **take part in** ~に参加する 動 分ける, 分かれる, 別れる
- **partially** 副 ①部分的に, 不十分に ②不公平に
- **participate** 動 参加する, 加わる
- **participation** 名 参加, 関与
- **particular** 形 ①特別の ②詳細な 名 事項, 細部, 《-s》詳細 **in particular** 特に, とりわけ
- **particularly** 副 特に, とりわけ
- **party** 名 ①パーティー, 会, 集まり ②派, 一行, 隊, 一味
- **pass** 動 ①過ぎる, 通る ②(年月が)たつ ③(試験に)合格する ④手渡す **pass away** 亡くなる **pass by** そばを通り過ぎる, 経過する 名 ①通過 ②入場券, 通行許可 ③合格, パス
- **passenger** 名 乗客, 旅客
- **passive** 形 ①消極的な, やる気のない ②(文法の)受動態の, 受け身の **passive vocabulary** 理解語彙
- **past** 形 過去の, この前の 名 過去(の出来事) 前 《時間・場所》~を過ぎて,

WORD LIST

~を越して 副 通り越して, 過ぎて
- **Pat** 名 パット《人名》
- **path** 名 ①(踏まれてできた)小道, 歩道 ②進路, 通路
- **patient** 形 我慢[忍耐]強い, 根気のある 名 病人, 患者
- **pattern** 名 ①柄, 型, 模様 ②手本, 模範 動 ①手本にする ②模様をつける
- **Paul** 名 ポール《人名》
- **pause** 動 中止する, 休止する
- **pay** 動 ①支払う, 払う, 報いる, 償う ②割に合う, ペイする 名 給料, 報い
- **payment** 名 支払い, 払い込み
- **peak** 名 頂点, 最高点 動 最高になる, ピークに達する
- **Peal** 名 ピール《人名》
- **peer** 動 じっと見る 名 ①同等の人, 同僚 ②貴族
- **pencil** 名 鉛筆
- **people** 名 ①(一般に)人々 ②民衆, 世界の人々, 国民, 民族 ③人間
- **per** 前 ~につき, ~ごとに
- **perceive** 動 気づく, 感知する
- **percent** 名 パーセント, 百分率
- **percentage** 名 パーセンテージ, 割合, 比率
- **perception** 名 認識, 知覚(力), 認知, 理解(力)
- **perfect** 形 ①完璧な, 完全な ②純然たる 動 完成する, 改良[改善]する
- **perfectly** 副 完全に, 申し分なく
- **perform** 動 ①(任務などを)行う, 果たす, 実行する ②演じる, 演奏する
- **performance** 名 ①実行, 行為 ②成績, できばえ, 業績 ③演劇, 演奏, 見世物
- **perhaps** 副 たぶん, ことによると
- **period** 名 ①期, 期間, 時代 ②ピリオド, 終わり
- **persimmon** 名 カキ(柿)
- **person** 名 ①人 ②人格, 人柄 in person (本人)自ら, 自身で
- **pet** 名 ペット, お気に入り 形 お気に入りの, 愛がんの 動 かわいがる
- **Peyton City** ペイトン市《地名》
- **Philippe Ariès** フィリップ・アリエス《フランスの中世社会研究を主とする歴史家, 1914-1984》
- **Philippines** 名 フィリピン《国名》
- **phone** 名 電話 動 電話をかける
- **photo** 名《略式》写真
- **photograph** 名 写真 動 写真を撮る
- **photographer** 名 写真家, カメラマン
- **physical** 形 ①物質の, 物理学の, 自然科学の ②身体の, 肉体の
- **physical activity** 身体活動
- **physical exercise** 体操
- **pianist** 名 ピアニスト
- **pianist-brother** 名 ピアニストの兄(弟)
- **piano** 名 ピアノ
- **pick** 動 ①(花・果実などを)摘む, もぐ ②選ぶ, 精選する ③つつく, つついて穴をあける, ほじくり出す ④(~を)摘み取る pick out えり抜く, 選び出す pick up 車で迎えに行く, 取り上げる, 手に取る pick up the language 言葉を覚える 名 ①《the -》精選したもの ②選択(権) ③つつくもの, つるはし
- **pickle** 名《-s》漬物, ピクルス 動 (塩水や酢に)漬ける
- **picture** 名 ①絵, 写真,《-s》映画 ②イメージ, 事態, 状況, 全体像 動 描く, 想像する
- **pie** 名 パイ pie chart 円グラフ
- **piece** 名 ①一片, 部分 ②1個, 1本 ③作品

- **pink** 形ピンク色の 名ピンク色
- **pistol** 名拳銃
- **place** 名①場所, 建物 ②余地, 空間 ③〈one's -〉家, 部屋 **at times and places** 思いもよらない時や場所で **in place of** ～の代わりに **take place** 行われる, 起こる **take the place of** ～の代わりをする 動 ①置く, 配置する ②任命する, 任じる
- **plain** 形 ①明白な, はっきりした ②簡素な ③平らな ④不細工な, 平凡な 副はっきりと, まったく 名高原, 草原
- **plan** 名計画, 設計(図), 案 動計画する
- **planet** 名惑星, 遊星
- **plant** 名 ①植物, 草木 ②設備, プラント, 工場 動植えつける, すえつける
- **play** 動 ①遊ぶ, 競技する ②(楽器を)演奏する, (役を)演じる 名遊び, 競技, 劇
- **player** 名 ①競技者, 選手, 演奏者, 俳優 ②演奏装置
- **playmate** 名遊び友達, 遊び仲間
- **plaza** 名広場, ショッピングセンター **central plaza** セントラルプラザ
- **pleasantly** 副楽しく, 心地よく
- **please** 動喜ばす, 満足させる 間どうぞ, お願いします
- **pleasure** 名喜び, 楽しみ, 満足, 娯楽 **(It's) my pleasure.** どういたしまして.
- **plus** 前～を加えて 形 ①正の, プラスの, 有利な ②上の部の 名 ①正符号, プラス, 正数 ②利息, 付加物 副その上に, さらに
- **pocket** 名 ①ポケット, 袋 ②所持金 動 ①ポケットに入れる ②着服する 形携帯用の, 小型の
- **point** 名 ①先, 先端 ②点 ③地点, 時点, 箇所 ④〈the -〉要点 **come to the point** 核心に触れる **on the point of** ～[～ing] まさに～しよう として **to the point** 要領を得た 動 ①(～を)指す, 向ける ②とがらせる **point out** 指摘する
- **pointed** 動 point (指す)の過去, 過去分詞 形先のとがった, 鋭い
- **Poland** 名ポーランド《国名》
- **policy** 名 ①政策, 方針, 手段 ②保険証券
- **polish** 動磨く, つやを出す, 磨きをかける 名つや出し, 磨き粉
- **pollution** 名汚染, 公害 **air pollution** 大気汚染
- **pool** 名 ①水たまり, プール ②共同出資 動共同出資する
- **poor** 形 ①貧しい, 乏しい, 粗末な, 貧弱な ②劣った, へたな ③不幸な, 哀れな, 気の毒な **poor conductor of heat** 熱を伝導しない
- **popular** 形 ①人気のある, 流行の ②一般的な, 一般向きの
- **popularity** 名人気, 流行
- **population** 名人口, 住民(数)
- **portion** 名一部, 分け前 動分配する
- **Portuguese** 形ポルトガル(人・語)の 名 ①ポルトガル人 ②ポルトガル語
- **Portville** 名ポートヴィル《都市名》
- **position** 名 ①位置, 場所, 姿勢 ②地位, 身分, 職 ③立場, 状況 動置く, 配置する
- **positive** 形 ①積極的な ②明確な, 明白な, 確信している ③プラスの, (写真が)ポジの 名 ①正数, プラス, 陽極 ②ポジ, 陽画
- **positively** 副明確に, 確かに, 積極的に
- **possibility** 名可能性, 見込み, 将来性
- **possible** 形 ①可能な ②ありうる, 起こりうる **as ～ as possible** できるだけ～ **if possible** できるなら
- **potential** 形可能性がある, 潜在

WORD LIST

的な 名可能性,潜在能力
- **pound** 名①ポンド《英国の通貨単位,記号》②ポンド《重量の単位,453.6g》動どんどんたたく,打ち砕く
- **pour** 動①注ぐ,浴びせる②流れ出る,流れ込む③ざあざあ降る
- **powerful** 形力強い,実力のある,影響力のある
- **practice** 名①実行,実践②練習③慣習④(医者・弁護士などの)業務⑤やり方,方法 in practice 実際には 動実行する,練習[訓練]する
- **praise** 動ほめる,賞賛する 名賞賛
- **precise** 形正確な,ち密な,ぴったりした
- **prefecture** 名県,府
- **prefer** 動(〜のほうを)好む,(〜のほうが)よいと思う
- **preference** 名好きであること,好み
- **preferred** 形好ましい
- **preparation** 名①準備,したく②心構え
- **prepare** 動①準備[用意]をする②覚悟する[させる]
- **present-day** 形今日の,現代の
- **presentation** 名①提出,提示②実演,プレゼンテーション
- **preserve** 動保存[保護]する,保つ
- **pressure** 名押すこと,圧力,圧縮,圧搾,電圧,重荷 high blood pressure 高血圧症 動圧力をかける
- **pretty** 形①かわいい,きれいな②相当な 副かなり,相当,非常に
- **prevent** 動①妨げる,じゃまする②予防する,守る,《〜 from …》〜が…できない[しない]ようにする
- **primary** 形第一の,主要な,最初の,初期の 名①第一のこと②予備選挙 primary school 小学校
- **print** 名①印刷(物),版画②(押された)跡,しるし 動①印刷する,出版[発行]する②しるす,残す
- **privacy** 名(干渉されない)自由な生活,プライバシー
- **probably** 副たぶん,あるいは
- **problem** 名問題,難問 No problem. いいですよ,どういたしまして,問題ない
- **process** 名①過程,経過,進行②手順,方法,製法,加工
- **produce** 動①生産する,製造する②生じる,引き起こす 名①生産額[物]②結果
- **producer** 名プロデューサー,製作者,生産者
- **product** 名①製品,産物②成果,結果 household product 家庭用品 local product 地場産品
- **production** 名製造,生産
- **productive** 形生産的な,豊富な
- **professional** 形専門の,プロの,職業的な 名専門家,プロ
- **profit** 名利益,利潤,ため 動利益になる,(人の)ためになる,役立つ
- **program** 名①番組,プログラム②計画,予定表 動①番組[計画表]を作る②(コンピュータの)プログラムを作る
- **programmer** 名プログラマー
- **progress** 名①進歩,前進②成り行き,経過 in progress 進行中で make progress 進歩[上達]する,前進する 動前進する,上達する
- **project** 名①計画,プロジェクト②研究課題 動①投影する,映写する②計画[企画]する③描く,予測する,見積もる
- **prominently** 副著しく,顕著に
- **promote** 動促進する,昇進[昇級]させる
- **pronunciation** 名発音
- **propel** 動推進する,駆り立てる

- **proper** 形 ①適した, 適切な, 正しい ②固有の
- **protect** 動 保護する, 防ぐ
- **protected** 形 保護された
- **protection** 名 保護, 保護するもの[人] rainforest protection laws 熱帯雨林保護法
- **proud** 形 ①自慢の, 誇った, 自尊心のある ②高慢な, 尊大な《be》proud of ～を自慢に思う
- **prove** 動 ①証明する ②(～であることが)わかる, (～と)なる
- **provide** 動 ①供給する, 用意する, (～に)備える ②規定する
- **psychologist** 名 心理学者, 精神分析医
- **psychology** 名 心理学, 心理, 性格
- **public** 形 ①公の, 一般の, 公共の ②知れ渡っている 名 社会, 公衆 in public 人前で, 公然と
- **pull** 動 ①引く, 引っ張る ②引きつける 名 ①引くこと ②縁故, こね
- **puppy** 名 子犬
- **purpose** 名 目的, 意図, 決意 on purpose わざと, 故意に to the purpose 目的にかなって 動 もくろむ, 企てる
- **Pusan** 名 釜山《韓国の都市》
- **push** 動 ①押す, 押し進む, 押し進める ②進む, 突き出る 名 押し, 突進, 後援
- **put** 動 ①置く, のせる ②入れる, つける ③(ある状態に)する ④putの過去, 過去分詞 put aside わきに置く put away 片づける, 取っておく put in 設置する, ～の中に入る put off 延期する, 要求をそらす, 不快にさせる, やめさせる put on (薬を)つける put up 建てる put up with ～を我慢する
- **puzzle** 名 ①難問, 当惑 ②パズル 動 迷わせる, 当惑する[させる]

Q

- **quality** 名 ①質, 性質, 品質 ②特性 ③良質
- **quantity** 名 ①量 ②《-ties》多量, たくさん
- **question** 名 質問, 疑問, 問題 come into question 問題になる, 議論される in question 問題の, 論争中の 動 ①質問する ②調査する ③疑う
- **quickly** 副 敏速に, 急いで
- **quietly** 副 ①静かに ②平穏に, 控えめに
- **quite** 副 ①まったく, すっかり, 完全に ②かなり, ずいぶん ③ほとんど not quite まったく～だというわけではない quite a bit 相当に quite [not] a few かなり多くの quite some time かなり長い間

R

- **rabbit** 名 ①ウサギ(兎), ウサギの毛皮 ②弱虫
- **race** 名 ①競争, 競走 ②人種, 種族 動 ①競争[競走]する ②疾走する
- **rain** 名 雨, 降雨 動 ①雨が降る ②雨のように降る[降らせる]
- **rainforest** 名 熱帯雨林 rainforest protection laws 熱帯雨林保護法
- **raise** 動 ①上げる, 高める ②起こす ③～を育てる ④(資金を)調達する 名 高める[上げる]こと, 昇給
- **ran** 動 run(走る)の過去
- **rancher** 名 牧場経営者 cattle rancher 牛の牧場主
- **randomly** 副 無作為に, 不規則に
- **range** 名 列, 連なり, 範囲 動 ①並ぶ, 並べる ②および
- **rapid** 形 速い, 急な, すばやい 名 《-s》急流, 早瀬

WORD LIST

- **rapidly** 副 速く,急速,すばやく,迅速に
- **rare** 形 ①まれな,珍しい,逸品の ②希薄な ③(肉が)生焼けの,レアの
- **rate** 名 ①割合,率 ②相場,料金 at any rate とにかく 動 ①見積もる,評価する[される] ②等級をつける
- **rather** 副 ①むしろ,かえって ②かなり,いくぶん,やや ③それどころか逆に would rather ~ than … …よりむしろ~したい
- **raw** 形 ①生の,未加工の ②未熟な 名生もの
- **reach** 動 ①着く,到着する,届く ②手を伸ばして取る 名手を伸ばすこと,(手の)届く範囲
- **react** 動 反応する,対処する
- **reaction** 名 反応,反動,反抗,影響
- **read** 動 読む,読書する read over ~に目を通す read through ~を読み通す
- **reader** 名 ①読者 ②読本,リーダー
- **reading** 動 read(読む)の現在分詞 名 読書,読み物,朗読
- **ready** 形 用意[準備]ができた,まさに~しようとする,今にも~せんばかりの get ready 用意[支度]をする 動 用意[準備]する
- **real** 形 実際の,実在する,本物の 副 本当に
- **realistic** 形 現実的な,現実主義の
- **realize** 動 理解する,実現する
- **really** 副 本当に,実際に,確かに
- **reason** 名 ①理由 ②理性,道理 動 ①推論する ②説き伏せる
- **reasonable** 形 筋の通った,分別のある
- **receive** 動 ①受け取る,受領する ②迎える,迎え入れる
- **recent** 形 近ごろの,近代の
- **recently** 副 近ごろ,最近

- **recognize** 動 認める,認識[承認]する
- **recommend** 動 ①推薦する ②勧告する,忠告する
- **recommendation** 名 ①推薦(状) ②勧告
- **record** 名 ①記録,登録,履歴 ②(音楽などの)レコード off the record 非公式で,オフレコで on record 記録されて,公表されて record keeper 記録係 動 ①記録[登録]する ②録音[録画]する
- **red** 形 赤い 名 赤,赤色 get into red 赤字になる,赤字を出す
- **red-faced** 形 赤い顔をした
- **reduce** 動 ①減じる ②しいて~させる,(~の)状態にする
- **refer** 動 ①〈 - to ~〉~に言及する,~と呼ぶ ②~を参照する,~に問い合わせる
- **reflect** 動 映る,反響する,反射する
- **refrigerator** 名 冷蔵庫
- **refuse** 動 拒絶する,断る 名 くず,廃物
- **regard** 動 ①〈~を…と〉見なす ②尊敬する,重きを置く ③関係がある 名 ①注意,関心,尊敬,好感 ③《-s》(手紙などで)よろしくというあいさつ in [with] regard to ~に関しては without regard to [for] ~を無視して
- **region** 名 ①地方,地域 ②範囲
- **regional** 形 地方の,局地的な
- **regular** 形 ①規則的な,秩序のある ②定期的な,一定の,習慣的な
- **relate** 動 ①関連がある,かかわる,うまく折り合う ②物語る
- **relationship** 名 関係,関連,血縁関係
- **relative** 形 関係のある,相対的な 名 親戚,同族
- **relatively** 副 比較的,相対的に

- **relaxation** 名息抜き、くつろぎ、緩和、弛緩
- **relay** 名交替、リレー、中継 動中継する、リレーする
- **release** 動①解き放す、釈放する ②免除する ③発表する、リリースする 名解放、釈放
- **reliable** 形信頼できる、確かな
- **reliance** 名①信頼、信用 ②依存 ③頼りになる人 reliance on ~への依存
- **relief** 名(苦痛・心配などの)除去、軽減、安心、気晴らし
- **relieve** 動(心配・苦痛などを)軽減する、ほっとさせる
- **rely** 動頼る、あてにする rely on ~に頼る、~を頼りにする
- **remain** 動①残っている、残る ②(~の)ままである[いる] 名《-s》①残り(もの) ②遺跡
- **remark** 名①注意、注目、観察 ②意見、記事、批評 動①注目する ②述べる、批評する
- **remember** 動思い出す、覚えている、忘れないでいる
- **remind** 動思い出させる、気づかせる
- **Renaissance Italy** ルネサンス期のイタリア
- **repeatedly** 副繰り返して、たびたび
- **replace** 動①取り替える、差し替える ②元に戻す
- **reply** 動答える、返事をする、応答する 名答え、返事、応答
- **report** 動①報告[通知・発表]する ②記録する、記事を書く 名①報告、レポート ②(新聞の)記事、報道
- **represent** 動①表現する ②意味する ③代表する
- **require** 動①必要とする、要する ②命じる、請求する
- **research** 名調査、研究 動調査する、研究する
- **researcher** 名調査員、研究者
- **resist** 動抵抗[反抗・反撃]する、耐える
- **resistant** 名抵抗者、反抗者
- **resort** 名①行楽地、リゾート ②頼みの綱、頼り 動①手段に訴える ②行く、通う
- **resource** 名資源、財源、手腕
- **respect** 名①尊敬、尊重 ②注意、考慮 with respect to ~について、~に関して 動尊敬[尊重]する
- **respectively** 副それぞれに、めいめい
- **respond** 動答える、返答[応答]する
- **respondent** 名応答者、回答者
- **response** 名応答、反応、返答
- **responsibility** 名①責任、義務、義理 ②負担、責務
- **responsible** 形責任のある、信頼できる、確実な
- **rest** 名①休息 ②安静 ③休止、停止 ④《the-》残り 動①休む、眠る ②休止する、静止する ③(~に)基づいている ④(~の)ままである
- **restroom** 名化粧室、洗面所
- **result** 名①結果、成り行き、成績 as a result その結果(として) as a result of ~の結果(として) 動(結果として)起こる、生じる、結局~になる
- **return** 動帰る、戻る、返す 名①帰還、返却 ②返答、報告(書)、申告 by return 折り返し in return (for ~) (~の)お返しに 形①帰りの、往復の ②お返しの
- **revolution** 名①革命、変革 ②回転、旋回
- **reward** 名報酬、償い、応報 動報いる、報酬を与える
- **re-written** 動 re-write (書き直す)の過去分詞

- **ribbon** 名 リボン(状のもの) 動 リボンをつける
- **rice** 名 米, 飯 rice ball おにぎり
- **rifle** 名 ライフル銃
- **right** 形 ①正しい ②適切な ③健全な ④右(側)の 副 ①まっすぐに, すぐに ②右(側)に ③ちょうど, 正確に right away すぐに right now 今すぐに, たった今 right on top of ~の真上に ①正しいこと ②権利 ③《the-》右, ライト ④《the R-》右翼
- **ring** 名 ①輪, 円形, 指輪 ②競技場, リング 動 ①輪で取り囲む ②鳴る, 鳴らす ③電話をかける
- **rise** 動 ①昇る, 上がる ②生じる 名 ①上昇, 上がること ②発生 give rise to ~を引き起こす
- **risk** 名 危険 at any risk どんな危険をおかしても, 何が何でも at the risk of ~の危険をおかして 動 危険にさらす, 賭ける, 危険をおかす
- **river** 名 ①川 ②(溶岩などの)大量流出
- **road** 名 ①道路, 道, 通り ②手段, 方法
- **rock and roll** ロックンロール《音楽》
- **rocky** 形 ①岩の多い ②ぐらぐら揺れる, ぐらつく
- **role** 名 ①(劇などの)役 ②役割, 任務 role model 模範になる人 take an active role 積極的な役割を担う
- **romance** 名 恋愛(関係・感情), 恋愛[空想・冒険]小説
- **roof** 名 ①屋根(のようなもの), 住居 動 屋根をつける
- **room** 名 ①部屋 ②空間, 余地
- **rose** 名 ①バラ(の花) ②バラ色 形 バラ色の 動 rise(昇る)の過去
- **Rosemont** 名 ローズモント《地名》
- **rounded** 形 丸い, 丸みを帯びた

- **route** 名 道, 道筋, 進路, 回路
- **row** 名 ①(横に並んだ)列 ②舟をこぐこと ③論争, 騒ぎ in a row 1列に, 連続して 動 ①1列に並べる ②(舟を)こぐ ③騒ぐ
- **rub** 動 ①こする, こすって磨く ②すりむく 名 摩擦
- **rubber** 名 ゴム, 消しゴム
- **rule** 名 ①規則, ルール ②支配 as a rule 一般に, 原則として make it a rule to ~することにしている 動 支配する
- **run** 動 ①走る ②運行する ③(川が)流れる ④経営する 名 ①走ること, 競走 ②連続, 続き ③得点
- **Russian** 名 ロシア(人・語)の 名 ①ロシア人 ②ロシア語
- **ryokan inn** 旅館

S

- **sacred** 形 神聖な, 厳粛な
- **sad** 形 ①悲しい, 悲しげな ②惨めな, 不運な
- **sadly** 副 悲しそうに, 不幸にも
- **safe** 形 ①安全な, 危険のない ②用心深い, 慎重な on the safe side 大事を取って 名 金庫
- **safely** 副 安全に, 間違いなく
- **safety** 名 安全, 無事, 確実
- **Sakura Hotel** さくらホテル
- **same** 形 ①同じ, 同様の ②前述の the same ~ as [that] ……と同じ(ような) 代 《the-》同一の人[物] 副 《the-》同様に
- **sand** 名 ①砂 ②《-s》砂漠, 砂浜
- **sandwich** 名 サンドイッチ 動 間にはさむ, 挿入する
- **Sarah** 名 サラ《人名》
- **sat** 動 sit(座る)の過去, 過去分詞
- **satisfactory** 形 満足な, 十分な

- **Saturday** 名 土曜日
- **saw** 動 ①see (見る) の過去 ②のこぎりで切る, のこぎりを使う 名 のこぎり
- **say** 動 言う, 口に出す that is to say すなわち They say ~. ~ということだ. to say nothing of ~ は言うまでもなく What do you say to ~? = はいかがですか. 名 言うこと, 言い分 間 さあ, まあ
- **saying** 動 say (言う) の現在分詞 名 ことわざ, 格言, 発言 old saying 古いことわざ
- **scan** 動 ざっと目を通す, 細かく調べる, スキャンする 名 スキャン, 精査
- **scare** 動 こわがらせる, おびえる 名 恐れ, 不安
- **scene** 名 ①光景, 風景 ②(劇の)場, 一幕 ③(事件の)現場
- **schedule** 名 予定, スケジュール 動 予定を立てる
- **scholarship** 名 ①奨学金 ②学問, 学識
- **school** 名 ①学校, 校舎, 授業(時間) ②教習所, 学部 ③流派 ④群れ
- **science** 名 (自然)科学, 理科, ~学, 学問
- **scientist** 名 (自然)科学者
- **scratch** 動 ひっかく, 傷をつける, はがし取る 名 ひっかき傷, かくこと
- **scream** 名 金切り声, 絶叫 動 叫ぶ, 金切り声を出す
- **screen** 名 ①仕切り, 幕, スクリーン, 画面 動 ①仕切る ②審査する ③上映する, 映画化する
- **sea** 名 海,《the ~ S-, the S- of ~》 ~海
- **search** 動 捜し求める, 調べる 名 捜査, 探索, 調査 job search 就職活動
- **seat** 名 席, 座席, 位置 動 着席させる, すえつける

- **second** 名 ①第2(の人[物]) ②(時間の)秒, 瞬時 at the last second 最後の最後で 形 第2の, 2番の 副 第2に 動 後援する, 支持する
- **secondary** 形 ①第2の, 2番目の ②二次的な
- **secure** 形 ①安全な ②しっかりした, 保証された 動 ①安全にする ②確保する, 手に入れる
- **see** 動 ①見る, 見える, 見物する ②(~と)わかる, 認識する, 経験する ③会う ④考える, 確かめる, 調べる ⑤気をつける come to see ~ が理解できるようになる I see. わかりました. Let me see. ええと。 see ~ as … ~を…と考える See you (later). ではまた。 you see あのね, いいですか
- **seek** 動 捜し求める, 求める seek out ~を捜し出す
- **seem** 動 (~に)見える, (~のように)思われる
- **seen** 動 see (見る) の過去分詞
- **seize** 動 ①ぐっとつかむ, 捕らえる ②襲う
- **select** 動 選択する, 選ぶ 形 選んだ, 一流の, えり抜きの
- **self-conscious** 形 自意識過剰の
- **self-sacrificing** 形 自己犠牲的な
- **sell** 動 売る, 売っている, 売れる sell out 売り切る, 裏切る
- **semiconductor** 名 半導体
- **send** 動 ①送る, 届ける ②手紙を出す ③(人を~に)行かせる ④《~+人[物など] + ~ing》~を(ある状態に)する send in 送付する, 提出する send for ~を呼びにやる
- **senior** 形 年長の, 年上の, 古参の, 上級の 名 年長者, 先輩, 先任者
- **sense** 名 ①感覚, 感じ ②《-s》意識, 正気, 本性 ③常識, 分別, センス ④意味 in a sense ある意味では make sense 意味をなす, よくわかる 動 感じる, 気づく

- **sensitive** 形 敏感な, 感度がいい, 繊細な
- **sent** 動 send（送る）の過去, 過去分詞
- **separate** 動 ①分ける, 分かれる, 隔てる ②別れる, 別れさせる 形 分かれた, 別れた, 別々の
- **series** 名 一続き, 連続, シリーズ
- **serious** 形 ①まじめな, 真剣な ②重大な, 深刻な,（病気などが）重い
- **seriously** 副 ①真剣に, まじめに ②重大に
- **server** 名 サーバー《コンピュータ》
- **service** 名 ①勤務, 業務 ②公益事業 ③点検, 修理 ④奉仕, 貢献 動 保守点検する,（点検）修理をする
- **set** 動 ①置く, 当てる, つける ②整える, 設定する ③（太陽・月などが）沈む ④（〜を…の状態に）する, させる ⑤setの過去, 過去分詞 **set aside** 取っておく, 確保する **set off** 出発する, 発射する **set to** 〜に着手する **set up** 立てる,（テントを）張る, 創設する,（商売などを〜として）始める 形 ①決められた, 固定した ②断固とした ③準備のできた 名 ①一そろい, セット ②受信機 ③（テニスなどの）セット ④舞台装置, セット
- **seven** 名 7（の数字）, 7人［個］形 7の, 7人［個］の
- **seventeen** 名 17（の数字）, 17人［個］形 17の, 17人［個］の
- **seventeenth** 名 17, 17人［個］形 17の, 17人［個］の
- **several** 形 ①いくつかの ②めいめいの 代 いくつかのもの, 数人, 数個
- **shaky** 形 ①震える, 揺れる ②あてにならない, 不確実な
- **shall** 助 ①《Iが主語で》〜するだろう, 〜だろう ②《I以外が主語で》（…に）〜させよう,（…は）〜することになるだろう **Shall I 〜?**（私が）〜しましょうか **Shall we 〜?**（一緒に）〜しましょうか。

- **shame** 名 ①恥, 恥辱 ②恥ずべきこと, ひどいこと 動 恥をかかせる, 侮辱する
- **shape** 名 ①形, 姿, 型 ②状態, 調子 動 形づくる, 具体化する **shape up** 具体化する, 調子がよくなる
- **share** 名 ①分け前, 分担 ②株 動 分配する, 共有する
- **sharp** 形 ①鋭い, とがった ②刺すような, きつい ③鋭敏な ④急な 副 ①鋭く, 急に ②（時間が）ちょうど
- **she** 代 彼女は［が］
- **sheet** 名 ①シーツ ②（紙などの）1枚
- **shelf** 名 棚
- **shelter** 名 ①避難所, 隠れ家 ②保護, 避難 動 避難する, 隠れる
- **Shimonoseki** 名 下関《都市名》
- **ship** 名 船, 飛行船 動 ①船に積む, 運送する ②乗船する
- **shirt** 名 ワイシャツ, ブラウス
- **shoe** 名《-s》靴 動（馬に）てい鉄をうつ
- **shoot** 動 ①（銃を）撃つ ②放つ, 噴出する ③（球技で）シュートする 名 ①芽, 若芽 ②射撃, 発射
- **shop** 名 ①店, 小売り店 ②仕事場 動 買い物をする
- **shopping** 動 shop（買い物をする）の現在分詞 名 買い物
- **shore** 名 岸, 海岸, 陸 **in shore** 岸近くに **off shore** 沖合いに **on shore** 陸に
- **short** 形 ①短い ②背の低い ③不足している **be short of** 〜が足りない 副 ①手短に, 簡単に ②不足して **run short** 不足する, 切らす 名 ①《the-》要点 ②短編映画 ③（野球で）ショート **for short** 略して **in short** 要約すると
- **shortly** 副 まもなく, すぐに
- **shot** 動 shoot（撃つ）の過去, 過去分詞 名 ①発砲, 銃撃 ②弾丸

- **should** 助 ~すべきである、~したほうがよい
- **shoulder** 名 肩 動 肩にかつぐ、肩で押し分けて進む
- **shout** 動 叫ぶ、大声で言う、どなりつける 名 叫び、大声、悲鳴
- **show** 動 ①見せる、示す、見える ②明らかにする、教える ③案内する show off 見せびらかす、目立とうとする show up 顔を出す、現れる 名 ①表示、見世物、ショー ②外見、様子
- **shown** 動 show（見せる）の過去分詞
- **shuttle** 名 定期往復便、折り返し運転、定期往復バス 動 往復する、左右に動く
- **shyly** 副 はにかんで、内気に
- **Siberia** 名 シベリア
- **sick** 形 ①病気の ②むかついて、いや気がさして
- **side** 名 側、横、そば、斜面 on the safe side 大事を取って side by side 並んで 形 ①側面の、横の ②副次的な 動 (~の)側につく、賛成する
- **sightseeing** 名 観光、見物 sightseeing spot 観光名所
- **sign** 名 ①きざし、徴候 ②跡 ③記号 ④身振り、合図、看板 動 ①署名する、サインする ②合図する
- **sign language** 手話
- **signal** 名 信号、合図、信号機 動 信号を送る、合図する
- **significant** 形 ①重要な、有意義な ②大幅な、著しい ③意味ありげな
- **silence** 名 沈黙、無言、静寂 in silence 黙って、沈黙のうちに 動 沈黙させる、静める
- **silent** 形 ①無言の、黙っている ②静かな、音を立てない ③活動しない
- **similar** 形 同じような、類似した、相似の 《be》similar to ~と似ている
- **similarly** 副 同様に、類似して、同じように
- **simple** 形 ①単純な、簡単な、質素な ②単一の、単独の ③普通の、ただの
- **simply** 副 ①簡単に ②単に、ただ ③まったく、完全に
- **since** 接 ①~以来 ②~だから 前 ~以来 副 それ以来 ever since それ以来ずっと long since ずっと以前に
- **single** 形 ①たった1つの ②1人用の、それぞれの ③独身の ④片道の 名 ①片道乗車券 ②（ホテルなどの）1人用の部屋 ③(-s)（テニスなどの）シングルス
- **sister** 名 ①姉妹、姉、妹 ②修道女
- **sit** 動 ①座る、腰掛ける ②止まる ③位置する
- **site** 名 位置、敷地、用地 動 （ある場所に建物を）設ける、位置させる
- **situation** 名 ①場所、位置 ②状況、境遇、立場
- **six** 名 6（の数字）、6人[個] 形 6の、6人[個]の
- **sixty** 名 60（の数字）、60人[個] 形 60の、60人[個]の
- **skill** 名 ①技能、技術 ②上手、熟練
- **skin** 名 皮膚、皮、革（製品） skin cancer 皮膚がん 動 皮をはぐ、すりむく
- **skip** 動 ①跳ぶ、軽く跳び越す ②（途中を）抜かす、飛ばす 名 ①軽く跳ぶこと、スキップ ②飛ばす[抜かす]こと
- **sky** 名 ①空、天空、大空 ②天気、空模様、気色
- **slap** 動 （平手、平たいもので）ぴしゃりと打つ 名 ①平手打ち ②スラッシュ、斜線記号
- **sleep** 動 ①眠る、寝る ②活動しない 名 ①睡眠、冬眠 ②静止、不活動
- **sleeping** 名 眠り、睡眠
- **sleeplessness** 名 不眠(症)

WORD LIST

- **slightly** 副 わずかに, いささか
- **slim** 形 ほっそりした, わずかな, 薄い 動 やせる, やせさせる, 細くなる
- **slogan** 名 スローガン, モットー
- **slow** 形 遅い 副 遅く, ゆっくりと 動 遅くする, 速度を落とす slow down 速度を落とす
- **slowly** 副 遅く, ゆっくり
- **small** 形 ①小さい, 少ない ②取るに足りない 副 小さく, 細かく
- **smile** 動 微笑する, にっこり笑う 名 微笑, ほほえみ
- **smoking** 動 smoke (喫煙する) の現在分詞 名 喫煙 形 喫煙している, 喫煙の
- **snack** 名 軽食, おやつ 動 軽食をとる
- **snow** 名 雪 動 雪が降る
- **snowflake** 名 雪片
- **snowshoe hare** 名 カンジキウサギ
- **so** 副 ①とても ②同様に, ~もまた ③《先行する句・節の代用》そのように, そう not so ~ as … …ほど~でない or so ~かそこら, ~くらい so as to ~するように, ~するために so ~ as to … …するほど~で so far as ~する限り so far これまでのところ so that ~するために, それゆえに~ so ~ that … あまり~なので… だ 接 ①だから, それで ②では, さて So what? それがどうした。どうでもいいではないか。
- **so-called** 形 いわゆる
- **soccer** 名 サッカー
- **social** 形 ①社会の, 社会的な ②社交的な, 愛想のよい social interaction 社会的交流
- **society** 名 ①社会, 上流階級, ~界 ②協会, 団体 ③交際, 人前
- **soda** 名 ①ソーダ《ナトリウム化合物》②ソーダ水, 炭酸水, 炭酸清涼飲料
- **soft** 形 ①柔らかい, 手ざわり [口あたり] のよい ②温和な, 落ち着いた ③ (処分などが) 厳しくない, 手ぬるい, 甘い
- **software** 名 ソフト (ウェア)
- **sold** 動 sell (売る) の過去, 過去分詞
- **solution** 名 ①分解, 溶解 ②解決, 解明, 回答
- **solve** 動 解く, 解決する
- **some** 形 ①いくつかの, 多少の ②ある, 誰か, 何か some time いつか, そのうち 副 約, およそ 代 ①いくつか ②ある人 [物] たち
- **somehow** 副 ①どうにかこうにか, ともかく, 何とかして ②どういうわけか
- **someone** 代 ある人, 誰か
- **something** 代 ①ある物, 何か ②いくぶん, 多少
- **sometimes** 副 時々, 時たま
- **somewhat** 副 いくらか, やや, 多少
- **somewhere** 副 ①どこかへ [に] ②いつか, およそ
- **song** 名 歌, 詩歌, 鳴き声
- **soon** 副 まもなく, すぐに, すみやかに as soon as ~するとすぐ sooner or later 遅かれ早かれ
- **sorry** 形 気の毒に [申し訳なく] 思う, 残念な
- **sort** 名 種類, 品質 a sort of ~のようなもの, 一種の~ 動 分類する
- **sound** 名 音, 騒音, 響き, サウンド 動 ①音がする, 鳴る ②(~のように) 思われる, (~と) 聞こえる 形 ①健全な ②妥当な ③(睡眠が) ぐっすりの 副 (睡眠を) ぐっすりと, 十分に
- **source** 名 源, 原因, もと
- **south** 名《the -》南, 南方, 南部 形 南の, 南方 [南部] の
- **space** 名 ①空間, 宇宙 ②すき間, 余地, 場所, 間 動 間を空ける

- **space shuttle** スペースシャトル
- **Spain** 名 スペイン《国名》
- **Spanish** 形 スペイン(人・語)の 名 ①スペイン人 ②スペイン語
- **speak** 動 話す、言う、演説する so to speak いわば speak out はっきり[遠慮なく]言う
- **speaker** 名 ①話す人、演説者、代弁者 ②スピーカー、拡声器 ③議長
- **speaking** 動 speak (話す)の現在分詞 形 話す、ものを言う 名 話すこと、談話、演説
- **special** 形 ①特別の、特殊の、臨時の ②専門の
- **specialist** 名 専門家、スペシャリスト
- **specialize** 動 ~を専門とする
- **specialized** 動 specialize (専門にする)の過去、過去分詞 形 専門の、分化した
- **specially** 副 特別に
- **species** 名 種、種類、人種
- **specific** 形 明確な、はっきりした、具体的な
- **specification** 名 ①明細 ②《-s》仕様書、スペック
- **sped** 動 speed (急ぐ)の過去、過去分詞
- **speed** 名 速力、速度 動 ①急ぐ、急がせる ②制限速度以上で走る、スピード違反をする speed ahead 加速前進して
- **spend** 動 ①(金などを)使う、消費[浪費]する ②(時を)過ごす
- **spending** 名 支出、出費
- **spent** 動 spend (使う)の過去、過去分詞 形 使い果たした、疲れ切った
- **spill** 動 こぼす、まき散らす spill out あふれ出す、こぼれる 名 こぼすこと、流出
- **spoke** 動 speak (話す)の過去
- **spoken** 動 speak (話す)の過去分詞 形 口語の
- **sport** 名 ①スポーツ ②《-s》競技会、運動会 in [for] sport 冗談で
- **spot** 名 ①地点、場所、立場 ②斑点、しみ hot spot 人気のある場所 on the spot その場で、ただちに sightseeing spot 観光名所 動 ①~を見つける ②点を打つ、しみをつける
- **spray** 名 ①スプレー ②小枝 insect spray 殺虫スプレー 動 吹きかける
- **spread** 動 ①広がる、広げる、伸びる、伸ばす ②塗る、まく、散布する 名 広がり、拡大
- **spring** 名 ①春 ②泉、源 ③ばね、ぜんまい hot spring 温泉 動 跳ねる、跳ぶ
- **square** 名 ①正方形、四角い広場、(市外の)一区画 ②2乗、平方 形 ①正方形の、四角な、直角な、角ばった ②平方の 動 ①四角[直角]にする ②2乗する
- **square kilometer** 平方キロメートル《距離の単位》
- **staff** 名 職員、スタッフ 動 配置する
- **stair** 名 ①(階段の)1段 ②《-s》階段、はしご
- **stand** 動 ①立つ、立たせる、立っている、ある ②耐える、立ち向かう stand by そばに立つ、傍観する、待機する stand for ~を表す、~を支持する、~を我慢する stand out 突き出る、目立つ 名 ①台、屋台、スタンド ②《the -s》観覧席 ③立つこと
- **standard** 名 標準、規格、規準 形 ①標準の ②一流の、優秀な
- **star** 名 ①星、星形の物 ②人気者 形 星形の
- **stare** 動 じっと[じろじろ]見る 名 じっと見ること、凝視
- **start** 動 ①出発する、始まる、始める ②生じる、生じさせる 名 出発、開始

WORD LIST

- **starter pistol** スターターピストル
- **starve** 動①餓死する, 飢えさせる ②熱望する
- **state** 名①あり様, 状態 ②国家, (アメリカなどの)州 ③階層, 地位 動述べる, 表明する
- **station** 名①駅 ②署, 局, 本部, 部署 **gas station** ガソリンスタンド 動部署につかせる, 配置する
- **statistics** 名統計(学)
- **status** 名①(社会的な)地位, 身分, 立場 ②状態
- **stay** 動①とどまる, 泊まる, 滞在する ②持続する, (〜の)ままでいる **stay away (from 〜)** (〜から)離れている, (〜を)留守にする **stay behind** 居残る, 留守番をする **stay on** 居残る, とどまる, (電灯などが)ついたままである **stay up** 起きている, 夜更かしする 名滞在
- **steal** 動①盗む ②こっそりと手に入れる, こっそりと〜する 名盗み, 盗品
- **step** 名①歩み, 1歩(の距離) ②段階 ③踏み段, 階段 **step by step** 一歩一歩, 着実に 動歩む, 踏む
- **stereo** 名ステレオ
- **stereotype** 名ステレオタイプ, 定型, 固定観念
- **stick** 名棒, 杖 動①(突き)刺さる, 刺す ②くっつく, くっつける ③突き出る ④(受け身形で)いきづまる **stick with** 〜を続ける
- **still** 副①まだ, 今でも ②それでも(なお) 形静止した, 静かな
- **stir** 動かす, かき回す **stir up** かき立てる 名動き, かき回すこと
- **stomach** 名①胃, 腹 ②食欲, 欲望, 好み
- **stood** 動 stand (立つ)の過去, 過去分詞
- **stop** 動①やめる, やめさせる, 止める, 止まる ②立ち止まる **stop by** (途中で)立ち寄る **stop over** 途中下車する 名①停止 ②停留所, 駅
- **store** 名①店 ②蓄え ③貯蔵庫, 倉庫 **in store** 蓄えて, 用意されて 動蓄える, 貯蔵する
- **story** 名①物語, 話 ②(建物の)階
- **straight** 形①一直線の, まっすぐな, 直立[垂直]の ②率直な, 整然とした 副①一直線に, まっすぐに, 垂直に ②率直に 名一直線, ストレート
- **strange** 形①知らない, 見[聞き]慣れない ②奇妙な, 変わった **strange to say** 不思議な話だが
- **straw** 名麦わら, ストロー
- **straw hat** 麦わら帽子
- **stream** 名①小川, 流れ ②風潮 動流れ出る, 流れる, なびく
- **stress** 名①圧力 ②ストレス ③強勢 動①強調する ②圧力を加える
- **stressful** 形ストレスの多い
- **stretch** 動引き伸ばす, 広がる, 広げる 名①伸ばす[伸びる]こと, 広がり ②ストレッチ(運動)
- **strict** 形厳しい, 厳密な
- **strong** 形①強い, 堅固な, 強烈な ②濃い ③得意な 副強く, 猛烈に
- **strongly** 副強く, 頑丈に, 猛烈に, 熱心に
- **student** 名学生, 生徒 **exchange student** 交換留学生
- **studio** 名①スタジオ, 仕事場 ②ワンルームマンション
- **study** 動①勉強する, 研究する ②調べる 名①勉強, 研究 ②書斎
- **stuff** 名①材料, 原料 ②もの, 持ち物 動詰める, 詰め込む
- **style** 名やり方, 流儀, 様式, スタイル **out of style** 流行遅れの
- **submit** 動①服従する, 服従させる ②提出する
- **substance** 名①物質, 物 ②実質, 中身, 内容

- **succeed** 動①成功する ②(〜の)跡を継ぐ succeed in 〜に成功する
- **success** 名成功, 幸運, 上首尾
- **such** 形①そのような, このような ②そんなに, とても, 非常に such as たとえば〜, 〜のような such 〜 as …の…のような such 〜 that …と とても〜なので… 代そのような人[物] as such 〜など
- **suddenly** 副突然, 急に
- **suffer** 動①(苦痛・損害などを)受ける, こうむる ②(病気に)なる, 苦しむ, 悩む
- **sufficient** 形十分な, 足りる
- **sugar** 名①砂糖 ②甘言, お世辞 動砂糖を入れる, 甘くする
- **sugar cane** サトウキビ
- **suggest** 動①暗示する ②提案する
- **suggestion** 名①提案, 忠告 ②気配, 暗示
- **suitable** 形適当な, 似合う, ふさわしい
- **suited** 形適した
- **sum** 名①合計 ②金額 動①合計する ②要約する
- **summer** 名夏
- **sumo** 名相撲
- **sun** 名《the –》太陽, 日
- **sunflower** 名ヒマワリ(向日葵)
- **sunlight** 名日光
- **sunny** 形①日当たりのよい, 日のさす ②陽気な, 快活な
- **Sunnydale** 名サニーデイル《都市名》
- **support** 動①支える, 支持する ②養う, 援助する 名①支え, 支持 ②援助, 扶養
- **suppose** 動①仮定する, 推測する ②《be -d to 〜》〜することになっている, 〜するものである
- **sure** 形確かな, 確実な, 《be – to 〜》必ず[きっと]〜する, 確信して for sure 確かに make sure 確かめる, 手配する, to be sure 確かに, なるほど 副確かに, まったく, 本当に
- **surface** 名①表面, 水面 ②うわべ, 外見 on the surface 外面は, うわべは
- **surprise** 動驚かす, 不意に襲う 名驚き, 不意打ち to one's surprise 〜が驚いたことに
- **surprised** 動 surprise (驚かす)の過去, 過去分詞 形驚いた
- **surprisingly** 副驚くほど(に), 意外にも
- **surrounding** 動 surround (囲む)の現在分詞 名《-s》周囲の状況, 環境 形周囲の
- **survey** 動①見渡す ②概観する ③調査する 名①概観 ②調査
- **survival** 名生き残ること, 生存者, 残存物
- **Swahili** 名スワヒリ語
- **swam** 動 swim (泳ぐ)の過去
- **swerve** 動急に向きを変える, 急カーブを切る
- **swim** 動泳ぐ swim around 泳ぎ回る swim off 泳ぎ去る 名泳ぎ
- **swimmer** 名泳ぐ人, 水泳選手
- **swimming** 動 swim (泳ぐ)の現在分詞 名水泳
- **swimsuit** 名(女性用)水着
- **swum** 動 swim (泳ぐ)の過去分詞
- **symbol** 名シンボル, 象徴
- **sympathize** 動同情する, 気の毒に思う, 賛同する
- **symptom** 名①兆候, 現れ ②症状
- **system** 名制度, 系統, 体系, 秩序だった方法, 順序

WORD LIST

T

- **T-shirt** 名 Tシャツ
- **table** 名 ①テーブル,食卓,台 ②一覧表 動 卓上に置く,棚上げにする
- **Taipei** 名 台北《台湾の首都》
- **take** 動 ①取る,持つ ②持って[連れて]いく,捕らえる ③乗る ④(時間・労力を)費やす,必要とする ⑤(ある動作を)する ⑥飲む ⑦food, 受け入れる Take a look. ちょっと見てごらん。 take a turn 交代する take after ~に似る take an active role 積極的な役割を担う take ~ into account ~を考慮に入れる take off 脱ぐ,離陸する,出発する take one's eyes off ~から目をそらす take out 取り出す,連れ出す,持って帰る take up 取り上げる,拾い上げる,やり始める,(時間・場所を)とる 名 ①取得 ②捕獲
- **taken** 動 take (取る) の過去分詞
- **talent** 名 才能,才能ある人
- **talk** 動 話す,語る,相談する talk back 口答えする 名 ①話,おしゃべり ②演説 ③《the -》話題
- **tall** 形 高い,背の高い
- **tap** 動 ①軽くポンとたたく,たたいて合図する ②栓を抜いて出す 名 ①軽くたたくこと ②蛇口,コック ③盗聴器 water tap 給水栓
- **tape** 名 テープ,接着テープ,巻尺 動 ①テープに録音[録画]する ②テープで貼る,ひもでくくる ③巻尺で測る
- **target** 名 標的,目的の物,対象 動 的[目標]にする
- **task** 名 (やるべき)仕事,職務,課題 動 仕事を課す,負担をかける
- **taste** 名 ①味,風味 ②好み,趣味 動 味がする,味わう
- **taught** 動 teach (教える) の過去,過去分詞
- **tax** 名 ①税 ②重荷,重い負担 動 ①課税する ②重荷を負わせる
- **tax collector** 税務署員
- **tea** 名 ①茶,紅茶 ②お茶の会,午後のお茶
- **teach** 動 教える
- **teacher** 名 先生,教師
- **team** 名 (競技の)組,チーム
- **tear** 名 ①涙 ②裂け目 動 裂く,破る,引き離す
- **tease** 動 いじめる,からかう,悩ます
- **technological** 形 技術上の,(科学)技術の
- **technology** 名 技術,テクノロジー Information Technology 情報技術,IT
- **teddy bear** テディーベア,ぬいぐるみのクマ
- **teen** 形 13～19歳の 名 13から19歳の人
- **teenager** 名 10代の人,ティーンエイジャー《13歳から19歳》
- **telephone** 名 電話,電話機 動 電話をかける,電話で話す
- **television** 名 テレビ
- **tell** 動 ①話す,言う,語る ②教える,知らせる,伝える ③わかる,見分ける I (can) tell you. 本当に,絶対。
- **temperature** 名 温度,体温
- **ten** 名 10(の数字),10人[個] nine out of ten 9割がた 形 10の,10人[個]の
- **tend** 動 ①(~の)傾向がある,(~)しがちである ②向かう,行く
- **tendency** 名 傾向,風潮,性癖
- **Tenjin** 名 天神《福岡市の繁華街》
- **tense** 形 緊張した,切迫した,ぴんと張った 名《文法で》時制
- **tent** 名 テント,天幕
- **tenth** 名 第10番目(の人・物),10日 形 第10番目の
- **term** 名 ①期間,期限 ②語,用語 ③《-s》条件 ④《-s》関係,仲 come

to terms with ～と合意に達する、～を甘受する in terms of ～の観点から on ～ terms with …… と～な仲である

- **terrible** 形恐ろしい、ひどい、ものすごい、つらい
- **terrified** 形おびえた、こわがった
- **Terry** 名テリー《人名》
- **test** 名試験、テスト、検査 動試みる、試験する
- **text** 名本文、原本、テキスト、教科書
- **than** 接～よりも、～以上に
- **thank** 動感謝する、礼を言う 名《-s》感謝、謝意 Thanks a million. ありがとう。 thanks to ～のおかげで
- **that** 形その、あの 代①それ、あれ、その［あの］人［物］②《関係代名詞》～である… that is (to say) すなわち That's it. それだけのことだ。 接～ということ、～なので、～だから so that …できるように 副そんなに、それほど so ～ that … 非常に～なので…
- **the** 冠①その、あの ②《形容詞の前で》～な人々 副《＋比較級、＋比較級》～すればするほど…
- **their** 代彼(女)らの、それらの
- **them** 代彼(女)らを［に］、それらを［に］
- **themselves** 代彼(女)ら自身、それら自身
- **then** 副その時(に・は)、それから、次に (every) now and then 時折、時々 from then on それ以来、その時 形その当時の
- **there** 副①そこに［で・の］、そこへ、あそこへ ②《-is［are］～》～がある［いる］ 名そこ
- **therefore** 副したがって、それゆえ、その結果
- **these** 代これら、これ 形これらの、この
- **they** 代①彼(女)らは［が］、それらは［が］ ②（一般の）人々は［が］
- **thick** 形厚い、密集した、濃厚な 副厚く、濃く 名最も厚い［強い・濃い］部分
- **thin** 形薄い、細い、やせた、まばらな 副薄く 動薄く［細く］なる、薄くする
- **thing** 名①物、事 ②《-s》事情、事柄 ③《one's -s》持ち物、身の回り品 ④人、やつ 《be》not my thing 私に向いていない
- **think** 動思う、考える
- **thinker** 名思想家、考える人
- **thinking** 動 think (思う) の現在分詞 名考えること、思考 形思考力のある、考える
- **third** 名第3(の人［物］) 形第3の、3番の
- **thirsty** 形①のどが渇いた ②渇望する get thirsty のどが乾く
- **thirty** 名30(の数字)、30人［個］ 形30の、30人［個］
- **this** 形①この、こちらの、これを ②今の、現在の 代①これ、この人［物］ ②今、ここ
- **those** 形それらの、あれらの in those days その当時 代それら［あれら］の人［物］ those living in Tokyo 東京に住む人々
- **though** 接①～にもかかわらず、～だが ②たとえ～でも 副しかし
- **thought** 動 think (思う) の過去、過去分詞 名考え、意見
- **thousand** 名①1000 (の数字)、1000人［個］ ②《-s》何千、多数 形①1000の、1000人［個］の ②多数の
- **threatening** 動 threaten (脅かす) の現在分詞 形①脅迫的な ②（天候などが）今にもくずれそうな
- **three** 名3(の数字)、3人［個］ 形3の、3人［個］の
- **three-day weekend** 3連休

216

WORD LIST

- **through** 前 ～を通して、～中を[に]、～中 副 ①通して ②終わりまで、まったく、すっかり get through 乗り切る
- **throughout** 前 ①～中、～を通じて ②～のいたるところに 副 初めから終わりまで、ずっと
- **thumb** 名 親指
- **thus** 副 ①このように ②これだけ ③かくて、だから
- **ticket** 名 切符、乗車[入場]券、チケット 動 ①札をつける ②交通違反の切符を切る
- **tie** 動 結ぶ、束縛する tie up ひもで縛る、つなぐ、拘束する、提携させる 名 ①結び(目) ②ネクタイ ③《-s》縁、きずな
- **tight** 形 堅い、きつい、ぴんと張った 副 堅く、しっかりと
- **time** 名 ①時、時間、歳月 ②時期 ③期間 ④時代 ⑤回、倍 all the time ずっと、いつも at a time 一度に、続けざまに (at) any time いつでも at one time かつては at times 時折 at the time そのころ、当時は at times and places 思いもよらない時や場所で behind time 遅刻して for a time しばらく for the time being 今のところは from time to time 時々 have a good time 楽しい時を過ごす in no time すぐに in time 間に合って、やがて lose track of time どのくらい時間がたったか分からなくなる quite some time かなり長い間 on time 時間どおりに Time is up. もう時間だ。 time off 仕事を休んだ時間、休暇 動 時刻を決める、時間を計る
- **tired** 動 tire (疲れる)の過去、過去分詞 形 ①疲れた、くたびれた ②あきた、うんざりした
- **to** 前 ①《方向・変化》～へ、～に、～の方へ ②《程度・時間》～まで ③《適合・付加・所属》～に ④《-+動詞の原形》～するために[の]、～する、～すること

- **today** 名 今日 副 今日(で)は
- **toe** 名 足指、つま先
- **together** 副 ①一緒に、ともに ②同時に
- **Tokyo** 名 東京《地名》 those living in Tokyo 東京に住む人々
- **told** 動 tell (話す)の過去、過去分詞
- **toll-free** 形 フリーダイヤルの、通話料無料の、料金のかからない
- **Tommy** 名 トミー《人名》
- **Tomo** 名 トモ《人名》
- **tomorrow** 名 明日 副 明日は
- **too** 副 ①～も(また) ②あまりに～すぎる、とても～
- **took** 動 take (取る)の過去
- **tool** 名 道具、用具、工具
- **top** 名 ①頂上、首位 ②こま right on top of ～の真上に 形 いちばん上の 動 ①頂上を覆う ②首位を占める ③(～より)優れる
- **topic** 名 話題、見出し
- **total** 形 総計の、全体の、完全な 名 全体、合計 動 合計する
- **totally** 副 全体的に、すっかり
- **touch** 動 ①触れる、さわる、～を触れさせる ②接触する ③感動させる 名 ①接触、手ざわり ②手法 in touch (with ～) (～と)連絡を取って
- **tough** 形 堅い、丈夫な、たくましい、骨の折れる、困難な
- **tour** 名 ツアー、見て回ること、視察 package tour パックツアー 動 (観光)旅行する、巡業する
- **tourism** 名 ①観光旅行、観光業 ②《集合的》観光客
- **tourist** 名 旅行者、観光客
- **toward** 前 ①《運動の方向・位置》～の方へ、～に向かって ②《目的》～のために
- **towards** 前 ①《運動の方向・位置》～の方へ、～に向かって ②《目的》～

のために
- **towel** 名 タオル
- **tower** 名 塔、やぐら、砦 動 ①そびえる ②抜き出る
- **towering** 形 高くそびえる
- **town** 名 町、都会、都市
- **track** 名 ①通った跡 ②競走路、軌道、トラック animal track 動物の足跡 lose track of time どのくらい時間がたったか分からなくなる 動 追跡する
- **trade** 名 取引、貿易、商業 動 取引する、貿易する、商売する come to be traded 取引されるようになる
- **trading** 名 商取引、貿易
- **traditional** 形 伝統的な
- **traditionally** 副 伝統的に、元々は
- **traffic** 名 通行、往来、交通(量)、貿易 動 商売する、取引する
- **train** 名 ①列車、電車 ②(〜の)列、連続 last train home 帰りの最終列車 動 訓練する、仕立てる
- **training** 動 train (訓練する)の現在分詞 名 ①トレーニング、訓練 ②コンディション、体調
- **translate** 動 ①翻訳する、訳す ②変える、移す
- **translator** 名 翻訳者、通訳者
- **transport** 動 輸送[運送]する 名 輸送、運送(機関)
- **transportation** 名 交通(機関)、輸送手段
- **travel** 動 ①旅行する ②進む、移動する[させる]、伝わる 名 旅行、運行
- **traveler** 名 旅行者
- **treasure** 名 財宝、貴重品、宝物 動 秘蔵する
- **treat** 動 ①扱う ②治療する ③おごる 名 ①おごり、もてなし、ごちそう ②楽しみ
- **tree** 名 ①木、樹木、木製のもの ②系図
- **trend** 名 トレンド、傾向
- **trial** 名 ①試み、試験 ②苦難 ③裁判 形 試みの、試験の
- **triangle** 名 ①三角形 ②トライアングル《楽器》
- **triangle-shape** 名 三角形の形状
- **tribe** 名 部族、一族 native tribes 先住民
- **trick** 名 ①策略 ②いたずら、冗談 ③手品、錯覚 attempt the tricks わざを試す 動 だます
- **trip** 名 ①(短い)旅行、遠征、遠足、出張 ②幻覚体験、トリップ 動 つまずく、しくじる
- **trouble** 名 ①困難、迷惑 ②心配、苦労 ③もめごと get into trouble 困ったことになる、トラブルに巻き込まれる 動 ①悩ます、心配させる ②迷惑をかける
- **truck** 名 トラック、運搬車 farm truck 農業用トラック 動 トラックで運ぶ
- **true** 形 ①本当の、本物の、真の ②誠実な、確かな come true 実現する
- **trust** 動 信用[信頼]する、委託する 名 信用、信頼、委託
- **try** 動 ①やってみる、試みる ②努力する、努める try on 試着してみる try out 実際に試してみる 名 試み、試し
- **Tsukiji fish market** 築地魚市場
- **tunnel** 名 トンネル 動 トンネルを掘る
- **turn** 動 ①ひっくり返す、回転する[させる]、曲がる、曲げる、向かう、向ける ②(〜に)なる、(〜に)変える take a turn 交代する turn around 回転する、振り返る turn away 向きを変える turn down (音量などを)小さくする、弱くする、拒絶する turn into 〜に変わる turn off (スイッチなどを)ひねって止める、消す turn on (スイッチなどを)ひねって

WORD LIST

つける, 出す **turn out** (明かりを)消す, 追い出す, (結局〜に)なる, 裏返しになる **turn out to be** 〜という結果になる, 〜であるということが分かる **turn over** ひっくり返る[返す], (ページを)めくる, 思いめぐらす, 引き渡す 名①回転, 曲がり ②順番 ③変化, 転換 **by turns** 交替に **in turn** 順番に

- **TV** 名 テレビ
- **twelfth** 名 第12(の人・物) 形 第12の, 12番の
- **twelve** 名 12(の数字), 12人[個] 形 12の, 12人[個]の
- **twentieth** 名《the –》第20(の人・物) 形《the –》第20の, 20番の
- **21st Century Swimsuit Company** 21世紀水着カンパニー
- **two** 名 2(の数字), 2人[個] 形 2の, 2人[個]の
- **two-week** 形 2週間
- **type** 名 ①型, タイプ, 様式 ②見本, 模様, 典型 動 ①典型となる ②タイプで打つ
- **typical** 形 典型的な, 象徴的な
- **typically** 副 典型的に, いかにも〜らしく

U

- **uh** 間 あー, えー, あのー
- **UK** 名《U.K.とも》イギリス(=United Kingdom)
- **ultimate** 名 最終段階, 究極 形 最終の, 究極の
- **umm** 間 うーん
- **unable** 形《be – to 〜》〜することができない
- **uncle** 名 おじ
- **uncomfortable** 形 心地よくない
- **uncommon** 形 珍しい, まれな
- **under** 前 ①《位置》〜のド[に] ②《状態》〜で, 〜を受けて, 〜のもと ③《数量》〜以下[未満]の, 〜より下の 形 下の, 下部の 副 下に[で], 従属[服従]して
- **underneath** 前 〜のドに, 〜真下に 副 下に[を], 根底は 名《the –》底部
- **understand** 動 理解する, わかる, 〜を聞いて知っている **make oneself understood** 自分の言っていることをわからせる
- **understanding** 動 understand (理解する)の現在分詞 名 理解, 意見の一致, 了解 形 理解のある, 思いやりのある
- **understood** 動 understand (理解する)の過去, 過去分詞
- **underwear** 名 下着(類)
- **undoubtedly** 副 疑う余地なく
- **uneasy** 形 不安な, 焦って
- **unexpected** 形 思いがけない, 予期しない
- **unfair** 形 不公平な, 不当な
- **unfamiliar** 形 よく知らない, なじみのない, 不案内な
- **unfriendly** 形 友情のない, 不親切な
- **uniform** 名 制服 形 (形・質が)同一の, 一定の
- **unique** 形 唯一の, ユニークな, 独自の
- **United Kingdom** 連合王国, 英国, イギリス《国》
- **United States (of America)** アメリカ合衆国
- **university** 名 (総合)大学
- **unless** 接 もし〜でなければ, 〜でなければ
- **unlike** 形 似ていない, 違った 前 〜と違って
- **unmistakably** 副 まぎれもなく
- **unpleasant** 形 不愉快な, 気にさ

わる、いやな、不快な
- □ **unpleasantly** 副 不愉快そうに
- □ **unpopular** 形 人気がない、はやらない
- □ **unscheduled** 形 予定外の
- □ **until** 前 ～まで（ずっと） until the last minute 最後まで 接 ～の時まで、～するまで
- □ **unwillingly** 副 不本意に、いやいや
- □ **up** 副 ①上へ、上がって、北へ ②立って、近づいて ③向上して、増して be up to ～する力がある、～しようとしている、～の責任［義務］である up and down 上がったり下がったり、行ったり来たり、あちこちと up to (最高)～まで 前 ①～の上(の方)へ、高い方へ ②(道)に沿って 形 上向きの、上りの 名 上昇、向上、値上がり
- □ **upload** 動 アップロードする
- □ **us** 代 私たちを[に] 略《US》アメリカ合衆国（=U.S./the United States）
- □ **USA** 《U.S.A.とも》アメリカ合衆国（=United States of America）
- □ **use** 動 ①使う、用いる ②費やす get used to ～に慣れる 名 使用、用途 be of use 役に立つ have no use for ～には用がない、～に我慢できない in use 使用されて it is no use ～ing ～してもむだだ make use of ～を利用［使用］する of no use 使われないで
- □ **used to** 助 (以前は)だった、(以前は)したものだ
- □ **useful** 形 役に立つ、有効な、有益な
- □ **usual** 形 通常の、いつもの、平常の、普通の as usual いつものように、相変わらず
- □ **usually** 副 普通、いつも(は)

V

- □ **vacation** 名 (長期の)休暇 paid vacation 有給休暇、年休 動 休暇を取る、休暇を過ごす
- □ **vacuum cleaner** 電気掃除機
- □ **Valerie** 名 ヴァレリー《人名》
- □ **value** 名 価値、値打ち、価格 economic value 経済的価値 of value 貴重な、価値のある 動 評価する、値をつける、大切にする
- □ **van** 名 (小型)トラック、バン
- □ **variation** 名 変化、変化に富むこと、ばらつき
- □ **varied** 動 vary (変わる)の過去、過去分詞 形 さまざまな、多様な
- □ **variety** 名 ①変化、多様性、寄せ集め ②種類
- □ **various** 形 変化に富んだ、さまざまの、たくさんの
- □ **vary** 動 変わる、変える、変更する、異なる
- □ **vegetable** 名 野菜、青物 形 野菜の、植物(性)の
- □ **vehicle** 名 乗り物、車、車両
- □ **venice** 名 ヴェネチア、ヴェニス《イタリアの都市》
- □ **very** 副 とても、非常に、まったく 形 本当の、きわめて、まさしくその
- □ **via** 前 ～経由で、～によって
- □ **victim** 名 犠牲者、被害者
- □ **victory** 名 勝利、優勝
- □ **video** 名 ビデオ、テレビ
- □ **video game** テレビゲーム
- □ **videotape** 名 ビデオテープ
- □ **view** 名 ①眺め、景色、見晴らし ②考え方、意見 動 眺める
- □ **vinegar** 名 ビネガー、酢
- □ **violin** 名 バイオリン
- □ **vision** 名 ①視力 ②先見、洞察力
- □ **visit** 動 訪問する 名 訪問

WORD LIST

- **visitor** 名 訪問客
- **vitally** 副 極めて(重大で)
- **vivid** 形 鮮明な, 真に迫った, 生き生きした
- **vocabulary** 名 ①語彙 ②単語集 active vocabulary 使用語彙 command of a basic vocabulary 基礎語彙力 passive vocabulary 理解語彙
- **voice** 名 ①声, 音声 ②意見, 発言権 動 声に出す, 言い表す
- **volume** 名 ①本, 巻, 冊 ②《-s》たくさん, 多量 ③量, 容積
- **volunteer** 名 志願者, ボランティア International Year of the Volunteer ボランティア国際年 動 自発的に申し出る
- **volunteering** 名 社会奉仕活動
- **vote** 名 投票(権), 票決 動 投票する, 投票して決める
- **vowel** 名 母音(字)

W

- **wage** 名 賃金, 給料, 応酬 動 (戦争・闘争などを)行う
- **wait** 動 ①待つ, 《-for ~》~を待つ ②延ばす, 延ばせる, 遅らせる ③《-on [upon] ~》~に仕える, 給仕をする
- **waiting room** 待合室
- **walk** 動 歩く, 歩かせる, 散歩する walk off 立ち去る walk over to ~の方に歩いていく 名 歩くこと, 散歩
- **wall** 名 ①壁, 塀 ②障壁 動 壁[塀]で囲む, ふさぐ
- **wander** 動 ①さまよう, 放浪する, 横道へそれる ②放心する
- **want** 動 ほしい, 望む, ~したい, ~してほしい 名 欠乏, 不足
- **warm** 形 ①暖かい, 温暖な ②思いやりのある, 愛情のある 動 暖まる, 暖める warm up 暖まる, ウォーミングアップする, 盛り上がる
- **warmth** 名 暖かさ, 思いやり
- **warm-up** 名 ウォーミングアップ, 準備運動
- **was** 動 《be の第1・第3人称単数現在 am, is の過去》~であった, (~に)いた[あった]
- **wash** 動 ①洗う, 洗濯する ②押し流す[される] wash out 洗い落とす, 押し流す, (試合などを)中止させる, 落第させる wash up 手(や顔)を洗う, 皿洗いをする, (波が)打ち上げる 名 洗うこと
- **watch** 動 ①じっと見る, 見物する ②注意[用心]する, 監視する watch out 警戒[監視]する 名 ①警戒, 見張り ②腕時計
- **water** 名 ①水 ②(川・湖・海などの)多量の水 動 水を飲ませる, (植物に)水をやる
- **water tap** 給水栓
- **wave** 名 ①波 ②(手などを)振ること 動 ①揺れる, 揺らす, 波立つ ②(手などを振って)合図する
- **way** 名 ①道, 通り道 ②方向, 距離 ③方法, 手段 ④習慣 all the way ずっと, はるばる, いろいろと by the way ところで, 途中で by way of ~ を通って, ~経由で give way 道を譲る, 譲歩する, 負ける in a bad way 悪い方向に in no way 決して~でない in the [one's] way (の)じゃまになって make one's way 進む, 行く, 成功する make way 道を譲る[あける] No way! とんでもない, on the [one's] way (to ~) (~への)途中で under way 進行中で work one's way up 徐々に上っていく
- **we** 代 私たちは[が]
- **wear** 動 ①着る, 着ている, 身につける ②疲れる, 消耗する, すり切れる 名 ①着用 ②衣類
- **weather** 名 天気, 天候, 空模様

Readings from the National Center Test for English

- **webbed** 形 水かきのある
- **website** 名 ウェブサイト
- **week** 名 週, 1週間
- **weekend** 名 週末 形 週末の
- **weight** 名 ①重さ, 重力, 体重 ②重荷, 負担 ③重大さ, 勢力 動 ①重みをつける ②重荷を負わせる
- **weight-loss program** 減量プログラム
- **weight-training** 名 ウエイトトレーニング
- **welcome** 間 ようこそ 名 歓迎 動 歓迎する 形 歓迎される, 自由に〜してよい You're welcome. どういたしまして. よくいらっしゃいました.
- **well** 副 ①うまく, 上手に ②十分に, よく, かなり as well なお, その上, 同様に 〜 as well as ……と同様に〜も get on well with (人)とうまくやっていく may well 〜するのももっともだ, 多分〜だろう Well done! よくできた. 間 へえ, まあ, ええと 形 健康な, 適当な, 申し分ない get well (病気が)よくなる 名 井戸
- **well-balanced** 形 均衡の取れた
- **well-rounded** 形 幅の広い, 多方面にわたる
- **well-roundedness** 名 幅の広さ
- **went** 動 go (行く)の過去
- **were** 動 〈be の2人称単数・複数の過去〉〜であった, (〜に)いた[あった]
- **West** 名 ウエスト《人名》
- **Western European** 西欧人
- **what** 代 ①何が[を・に] ②《関係代名詞》〜するところのもの[こと] what about 〜はどうですか What (〜) for? 何のために, なぜ what if もし〜だったらどうなるだろうか What's up? 何があったのですか. やあ, どうですか. 形 ①何の, どんな ②なんと ③〜するだけの 副 いかに, どれほど
- **wheel** 名 ①輪, 車輪, 《the -》ハンドル ②旋回 動 ①回転する[させる] ②〜を押す
- **when** 副 ①いつ ②《関係副詞》〜するところの, 〜するとその時, 〜するとき 接 〜の時, 〜するとき 代 いつ
- **whenever** 接 ①〜するときはいつでも, 〜するたびに ②いつ〜しても
- **where** 副 ①どこに[で] ②《関係副詞》〜するところの, そしてそこで, 〜するところ 接 〜なところに[へ], 〜するところに[へ] 代 ①どこ, どの点 ②〜するところの
- **whether** 接 〜かどうか, 〜かまたは…, 〜であろうとなかろうと
- **which** 形 ①どちらの, どの, どれでも ②どんな〜でも, そしてこの 代 ①どちら, どれ, どの人[物] ②《関係代名詞》〜するところの at which = when in which = where/when on which = when
- **while** 接 ①〜の間(に), 〜する間(に) ②一方, 〜なのに 名 しばらくの間, 一定の時 for a while しばらくの間, 少しの間
- **white** 形 ①白い, (顔色などが)青ざめた ②白人の 名 白, 白色
- **white-haired** 形 白髪の
- **who** 代 ①誰が[は], どの人 ②《関係代名詞》〜するところの(人)
- **whole** 形 全体の, すべての, 完全な, 満〜, 丸〜 名 《the -》全体, 全部 as a whole 全体として, 概して, 総じて on the whole 全体として見ると
- **whom** 代 ①誰を[に] ②《関係代名詞》〜するところの人, そしてその人を
- **whose** 代 ①誰の ②《関係代名詞》(〜の)…するところの
- **why** 副 ①なぜ, どうして ②《関係副詞》〜するところの(理由) Why don't you 〜? 〜しませんか. Why not? どうしてだめなのですか. いいですとも. 間 ①おや, まあ ②

WORD LIST

もちろん, なんだって ③ええと
- **wide** 形幅の広い, 広範囲の, 幅が~ある 副広く, 大きく開いて
- **widely** 副広く, 広範囲にわたって
- **widen** 動広くなる[する], 大きく開く
- **wild** 形①野生の ②荒涼として ③荒っぽい ④奇抜な
- **will** 動~だろう, ~しよう, する(つもりだ) Will you ~? ~してくれませんか 名決意, 意図 battle of wills 意地の張り合い
- **willing** 形①喜んで~する, ~しても構わない, いとわない ②自分から進んで行う 《be》 willing to 進んで~する
- **willingness** 名意欲, 快く~すること
- **wind** 名①風 ②うねり, 一巻き 動巻く, からみつく, うねる
- **windy** 形①風の吹く, 風の強い ②激しい
- **winner** 名勝利者, 成功者
- **winning** 動win(勝つ)の現在分詞 名勝つこと, 勝利, 《-s》賞金 形勝った, 優勝の
- **winter** 名冬 動冬を過ごす
- **wisdom** 名知恵, 賢明(さ)
- **wish** 動望む, 願う, (~であればよいと)思う 名(心からの)願い
- **with** 前①《同伴・付属・所属》~と一緒に, ~を身につけて, ~とともに ②《様態》~(の状態)で, ~して ③《手段・道具》~で, ~を使って with respect to ~について, ~に関して
- **within** 前①~の中[内]に, ~の内部に ②~以内で, ~を越えないで 副中[内]へ[に], 内部に 名内部
- **without** 前~なしで, ~がなく, ~しないで not [never] … without ~ing ~せずに…しない, ~すれば必ず…する
- **witness** 名①証拠, 証言 ②目撃者 動①目撃する ②証言する
- **wolf** 名オオカミ(狼)
- **wolverine** 名クズリ(屈狸, 貂熊)
- **wolves** 名wolf(オオカミ)の複数
- **woman** 名(成人した)女性, 婦人
- **women** 名woman(女性)の複数
- **won** 動win(勝つ)の過去, 過去分詞
- **wonder** 動①不思議に思う, (~に)驚く ②(~かしらと)思う 名驚き(の念), 不思議なもの
- **wonderful** 形驚くべき, すばらしい, すてきな
- **wood** 名①《しばしば-s》森, 林 ②木材, まき
- **wooden** 形木製の, 木でできた
- **wool** 名羊毛, 毛糸, 織物, ウール
- **woolly** 形毛に覆われた, 毛の多い, 羊毛のような
- **word** 名①語, 単語 ②ひと言 ③《one's-》約束 in other words 言い換えれば
- **wore** 動wear(着ている)の過去
- **work** 動①働く, 勉強する, 取り組む ②機能[作用]する, うまくいく get to work 仕事を始める work on ~で働く, ~に取り組む, ~を説得する, ~に効く work one's way up 徐々に上っていく work out 算出する, (問題を)解く, 理解する, (合計が~に)なる, ~の結果になる, 体を鍛える 名①仕事, 勉強 ②職 ③作品 at work 働いて, 仕事中で, (機械が)稼動中で out of work 失業して
- **worker** 名働く人, 労働者
- **working** 動work(働く)の現在分詞 形働く, 作業の, 実用的な
- **workplace** 名職場, 仕事場
- **world** 名《the-》世界, ~界
- **worldwide** 形世界的な, 世界中に広まった, 世界規模の 副世界中に[で], 世界的に

- **worn** 動 wear (着ている)の過去分詞 形 ①すり切れた, 使い古した ②やつれた, 疲れた
- **worried** 動 worry (悩む)の過去, 過去分詞 形 心配そうな, 不安げな
- **worry** 動 悩む, 悩ませる, 心配する[させる] 名 苦労, 心配
- **would** 動《willの過去》①~するだろう, ~するつもりだ ②~したものだ would like ~がほしい would like to ~したいと思う Would you ~? ~してくださいませんか, Would you like ~? ~はいかがですか。
- **wound** 名 傷 動 ①負傷させる, (感情を)害する ②wind (巻く)の過去, 過去分詞
- **wow** 間《驚き, 喜び, 苦痛などを表して》わあ！, ああ！
- **wrap** 動 包む, 巻く, くるむ, 覆い隠す 名 包み
- **Wright** 名 ライト《人名》
- **wrinkle** 名 しわ 動 しわが寄る, しわを寄せる
- **write** 動 書く, 手紙を書く write down 書き留める
- **writer** 名 書き手, 作家
- **written** 動 write (書く)の過去分詞 形 文書の, 書かれた
- **wrong** 形 ①間違った, (道徳上)悪い ②調子が悪い, 故障した something is wrong with ~はどこか具合が悪い 副 間違って go wrong 失敗する, 道を踏みはずす, 調子が悪くなる 名 不正, 悪事
- **wrote** 動 write (書く)の過去
- **WXRP Channel 19** WXRP 19 チャンネル《テレビ局名》

Y

- **Yamanashi** 名 山梨《県名》
- **yard** 名 ①庭, 構内, 仕事場 ②ヤード《長さの単位。約91cm》
- **yeah** 間 うん, そうだね
- **year** 名 ①年, 1年 ②学年, 年度 ③~歳 for years 何年も
- **-year-old** 名 ~歳(の子ども)
- **yell** 動 大声をあげる, わめく 名 わめき声, 叫び
- **yellow** 形 黄色の 名 黄色
- **yes** 副 はい, そうです 名 肯定の言葉［返事］
- **yet** 副 ①《否定文で》まだ~(ない[しない]) ②《疑問文で》もう ③《肯定文で》まだ, 今もなお and yet それなのに, それにもかかわらず 接 それにもかかわらず, しかし, けれども
- **you** 代 ①あなた(方)は［が］, あなた(方)を[に] ②(一般に)人は
- **young** 形 若い, 幼い, 青年の
- **your** 代 あなた(方)の
- **youth** 名 若さ, 元気, 若者 youth culture 若者文化
- **youthful** 形 若々しい
- **Yuki** 名 有希《人名》
- **Yumiko** 名 由美子《人名》

Z

- **zoo** 名 動物園

ラダーシリーズ
Readings from the National Center Test for English
センター英語の長文を読もう

2010 年 4 月 6 日　第 1 刷発行

編　者　IBC パブリッシング

発行者　浦　　晋亮

発行所　IBC パブリッシング株式会社
　　　　〒162-0804 東京都新宿区中里町 29 番 3 号
　　　　菱秀神楽坂ビル 9 F
　　　　Tel. 03-3513-4511　Fax. 03-3513-4512
　　　　www.ibcpub.co.jp

© IBC Publishing, Inc. 2010

印刷　株式会社シナノ
装丁　伊藤 理恵
組版データ　Adobe Caslon Pro Regular + Frutiger 75 Black

落丁本・乱丁本は、小社宛にお送りください。送料小社負担にてお取り替えいたします。本書の無断複写 (コピー) は著作権法上での例外を除き禁じられています。

Printed in Japan
ISBN 978-4-7946-0034-9